# Heidi's Hoodles, The Trendy Doodles!

## Hand-Drawn Doodles for Adult Coloring and Relaxation

by Heidi M. Limburg

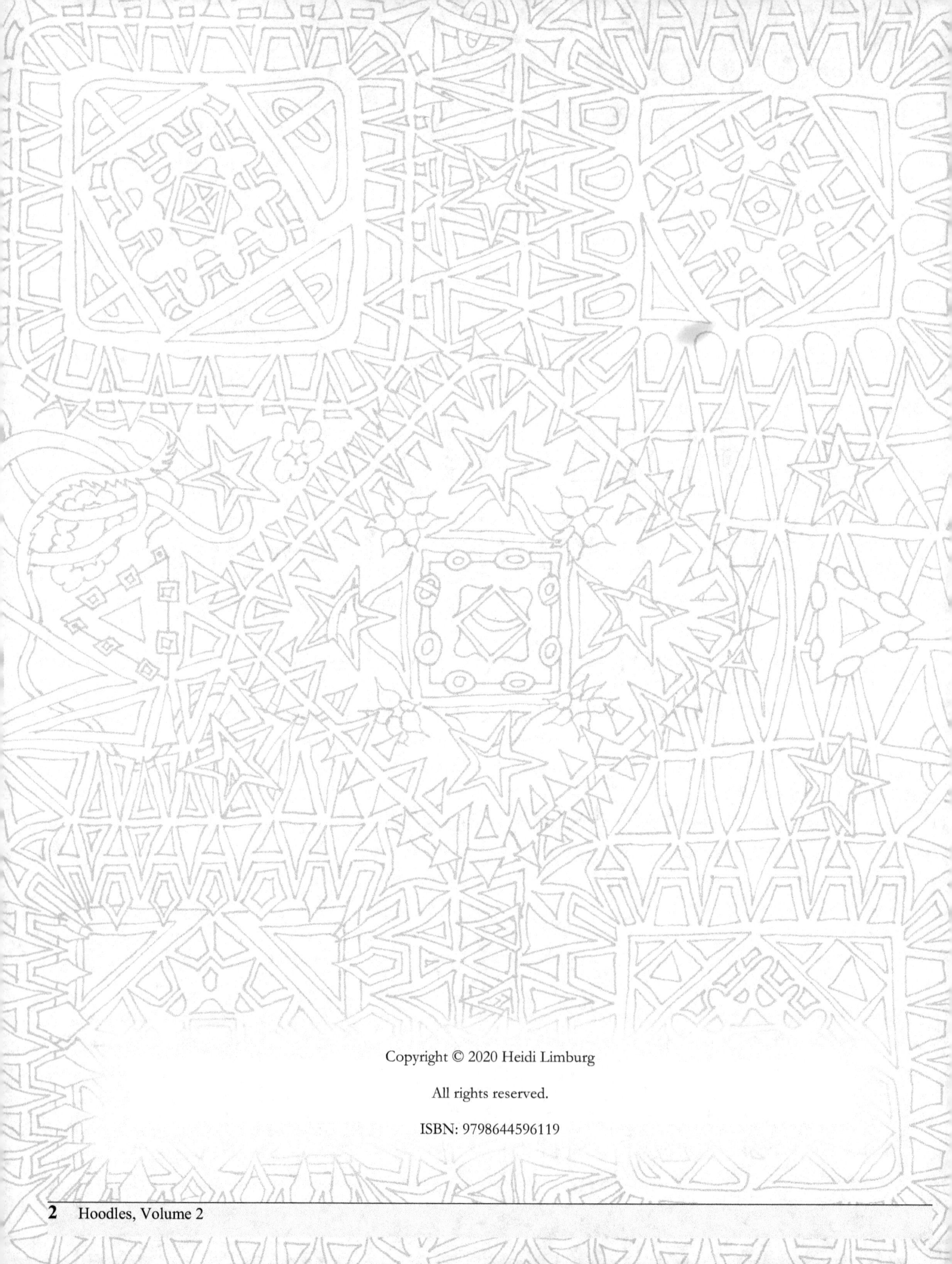

Copyright © 2020 Heidi Limburg

All rights reserved.

ISBN: 9798644596119

# About The Colorist

This book was colored by _____

In the city of _____

From the dates of _____ to _____

With help from the following colorists:

# Doodle Space

This book is dedicated to my sisters:

*Margaret McLaren Hoopingarner*

and

*Lisa Joy Limburg-Weber*

# Coloring Through COVID

Dear Reader,

This book was mostly ready to go in the summer of 2018. At some point, however, I became overwhelmed by the technicalities of figuring out the best dpi (dots per inch) to use when scanning my images and what software application to use to assemble the book. I had previously used the highest dpi of 1200 dots per square inch; however, the resulting file size crashed the program I used to assemble the book almost every time I opened it up. I tried scanning my images at a lower resolution but did not much like how they looked when I printed them out. In addition, Amazon stopped using Create Space and had sent an e-mail asking me to transfer my publishing endeavors to Kindle Direct Publishing. All of this combined felt like too much to deal with, and my Hoodles 2 project got relegated to the dusty basement of my mind, where it sat in the corner, cross-legged, glaring at me accusingly whenever I thought about it. For the sake of clarity, let's call this character "Bad Hoodles".

For my day job, I was completing substance abuse screenings over the phone and making referrals to treatment. My cubicle was in a large walk-out basement room next to a lovely outdoor walking trail. One day, one of my co-workers from a different department came over to visit with a tiny, flee-ridden (as it turned out) bundle of fur in his arms. He had rescued a kitten from the underside of another co-worker's car. She had heard it meowing when she pulled in to work, and had obtained his help to extract it. It had been sheltering in the wheel well for

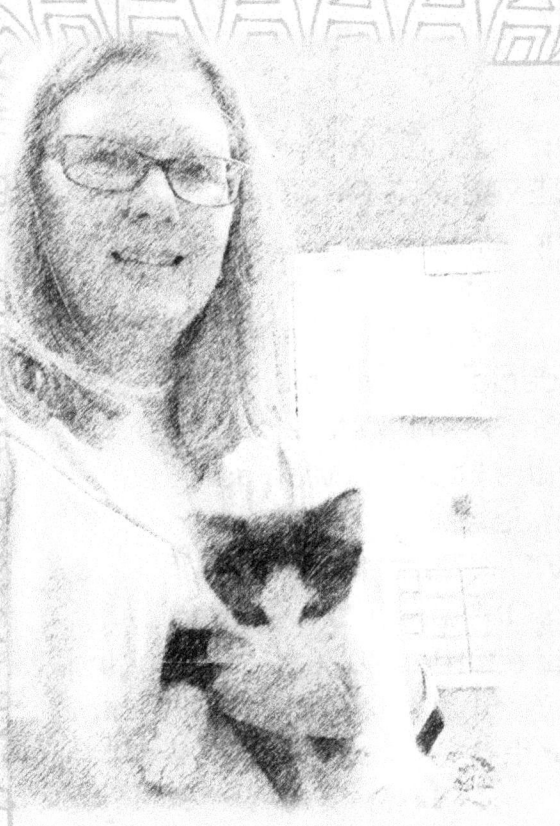

warmth and had clung for dear life in a journey over two highways that ended in our parking lot. I was only planning to hold the little furball for a minute, but as soon as he was in my arms, my heart melted and I was helpless to resist. To make a long story short, Oliver Simon Rose is now a member of my little family and will be turning 2 this June.

Speaking of my family, my daughter was warming up to her final year of elementary school last fall when I transferred to an administrative position within my agency. One of my favorite responsibilities is to publish a quarterly newsletter using Microsoft Publisher. The months were starting to blur together, and I only occasionally thought about Bad Hoodles, although when I did, it was in that same corner with the same accusatory glare. Then COVID happened.

I first read about COVID-19, the deadly coronavirus that has spread across the world, in January. It initially seemed like a distant problem. It was in China, and I was in Michigan. However, as we all know by now, it did eventually spread to the United States. The first two positive cases were identified in my state on March 10. The same day, governor Gretchen Whitmer issued executive order 2020-4, declaring a state of emergency across the state. That Friday, a general announcement was made at work, directing all staff to pack up and work from home for the next three weeks to help stop

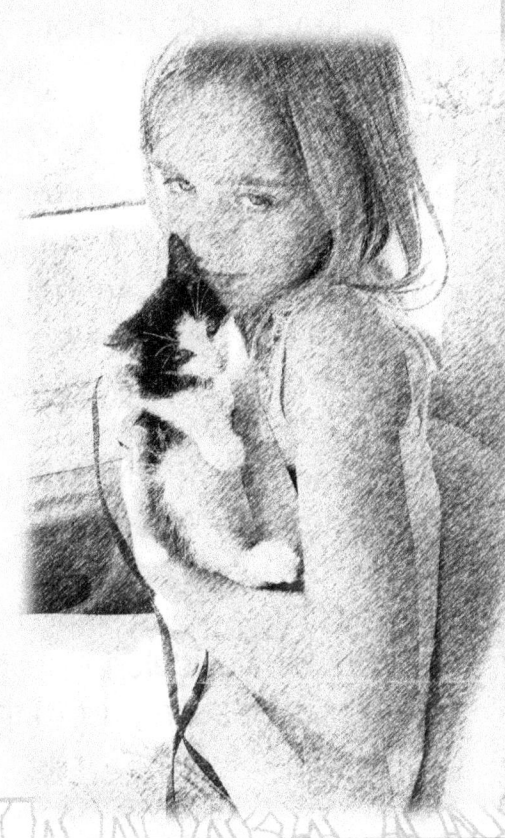

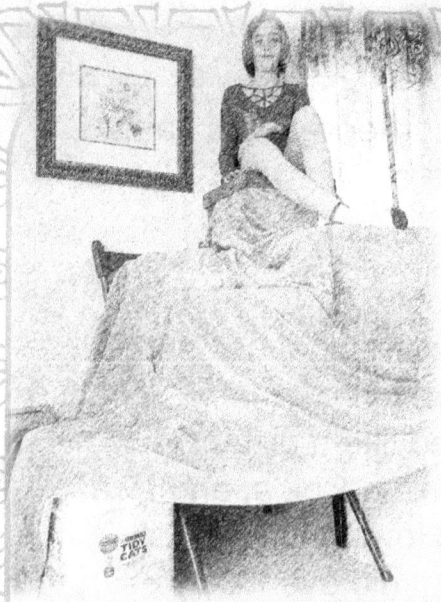

the spread of the virus.

My supervisor had her team report to work on Monday in order to wrap things up. I was one of the last employees to leave the building that day. I packed up all of the snacks from my cupboard and the break room refrigerator. I placed my two large-screen monitors into cloth grocery bags, and one of our tech guys helped me carry them to my car. That evening, I sorted through the various cords and connectors in order to set them up to work with my laptop, keyboard and mouse. I was ready to go in my home office by Tuesday morning.

The same Friday, an announcement was received from the public school system, stating that school would be closed until at least the end of the month. We settled into a work-at-home routine. My daughter did some reading and math every day. Her preferred activity once schoolwork was completed was building forts and listening to audiobooks and coloring or playing with Legos while in (or on) them.

On March 23, Governor Whitmer issued Executive Order 2020-21, directing all residents to "stay home and stay safe." On April 1, she issued Executive Order 2020-33, which declared both a state of emergency and a state of disaster across the State of Michigan, due to thousands of new confirmed cases of COVID-19 and hundreds of deaths. On April 9, she issued Executive Order 2020-42, extending the stay-at-home order to the end of the month.

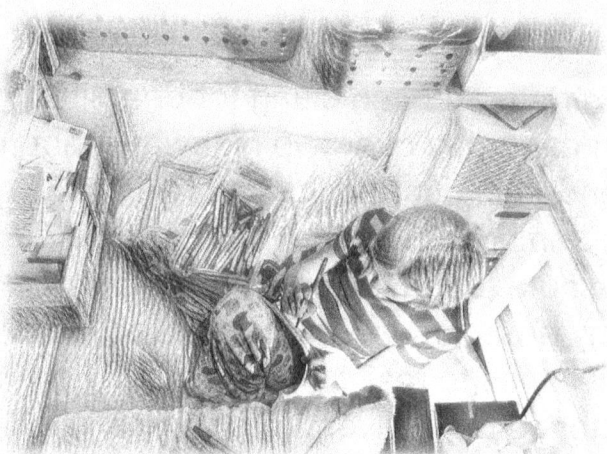

My family celebrated Easter Sunday together virtually over Zoom. My sister, Lisa, was the hostess and set up a camera at her dining room table so the rest of us could converse while enjoying the sight of her, her husband and three children eating ham, mashed potatoes and a lamb-shaped cake while eating our own meals (or snacks) at home.

I wore an improvised mask for the first time on April 16, for a trip to the grocery store to get supplies for my daughter's birthday cake.  The following day, we celebrated her 11th birthday by opening gifts and baking an angel food cake, which we frosted with whipped topping mixed with crushed pineapple.  She also enjoyed a long, Zoom-enabled playdate with two of her cousins and later, another virtual playdate with a friend.

While sheltering at home, we spent a lot of our free time coloring pictures from my first Hoodles book while listening to some of our favorite audiobooks for young adults, including the *Masterminds* series by Gordon Korman and the *Genius Files* series by Dan Gutman (both available on Hoopla, a free digital library app).  This got me thinking about the second, unfinished, book.  Today, I finally decided to do something about that.  While my daughter played with her newly downloaded game of Minecraft in her room, I re-scanned each of my "Hoodles 2" doodles at 1200 dpi. As this process was quite time consuming, I worked on my Spanish skills on Duolingo (a free language learning app) between scans.

And if you're reading this now, you know I was finally successful in getting my second coloring book out to print.  Bad Hoodles, no longer in my mental basement, has become a satisfied copy of Good Hoodles AKA "Hoodles 2," and is sitting in your hands right now, waiting to be colored.

If this book provides you with a few hours of quiet relaxation and a sense of personal accomplishment when you complete a picture, then I've achieved what I set out to do.

I wish you many happy hours of coloring, both this summer and in the years to come!

Happy Hoodling,


Heidi Limburg
April 19, 2020

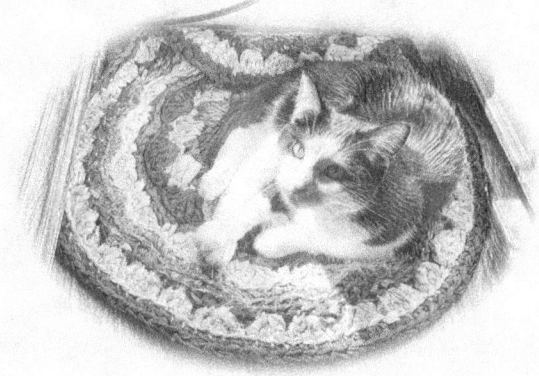

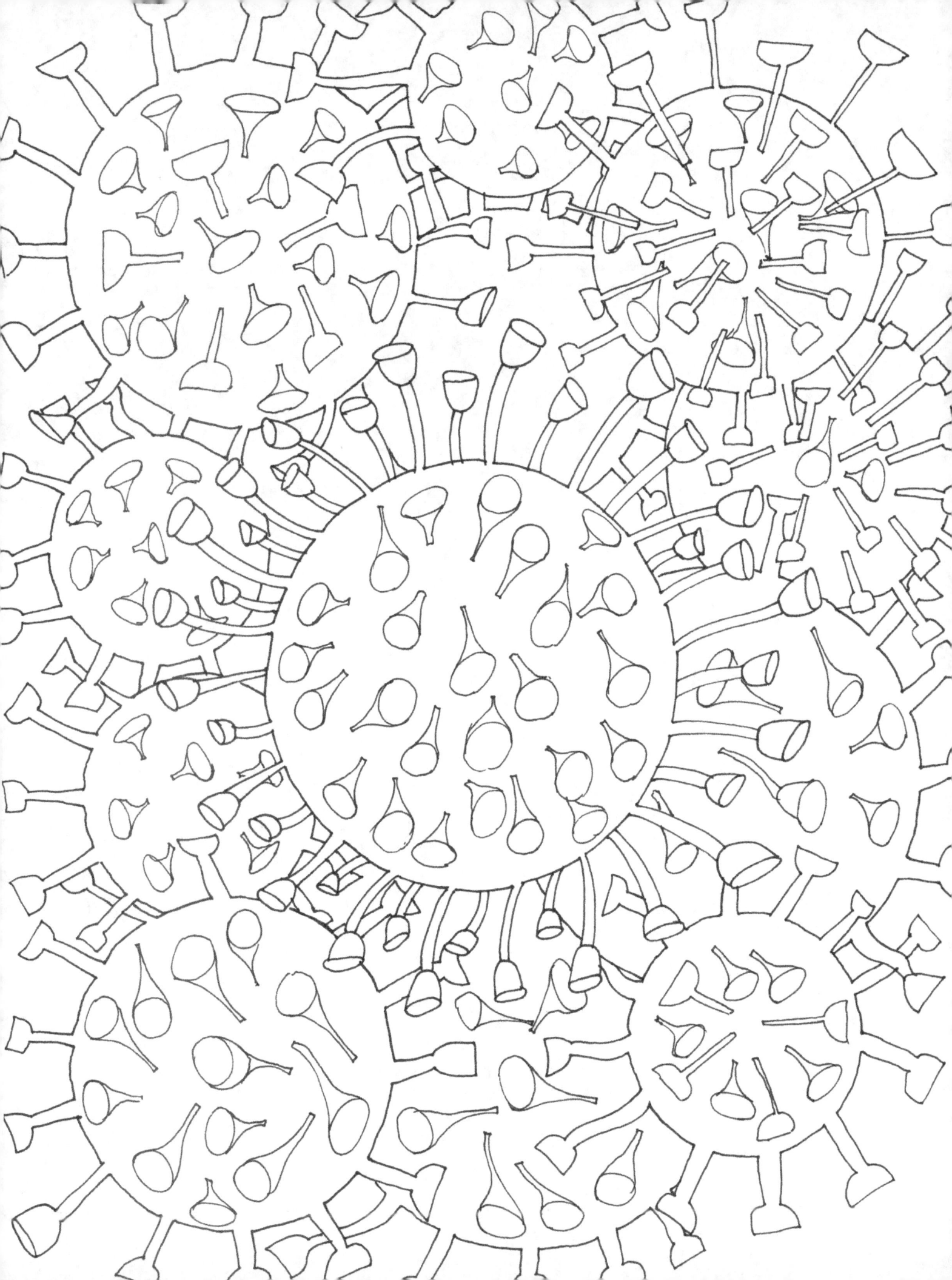

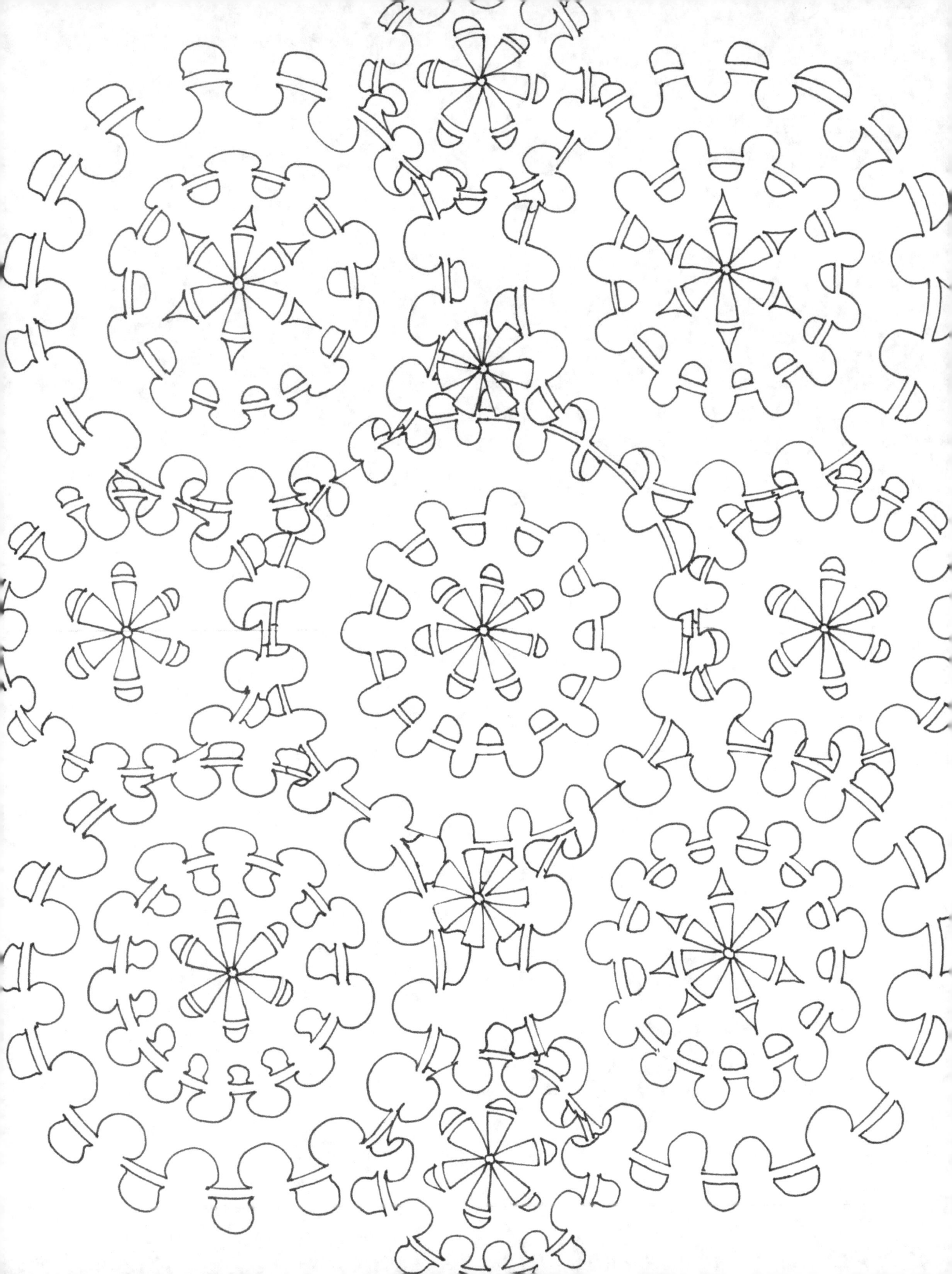

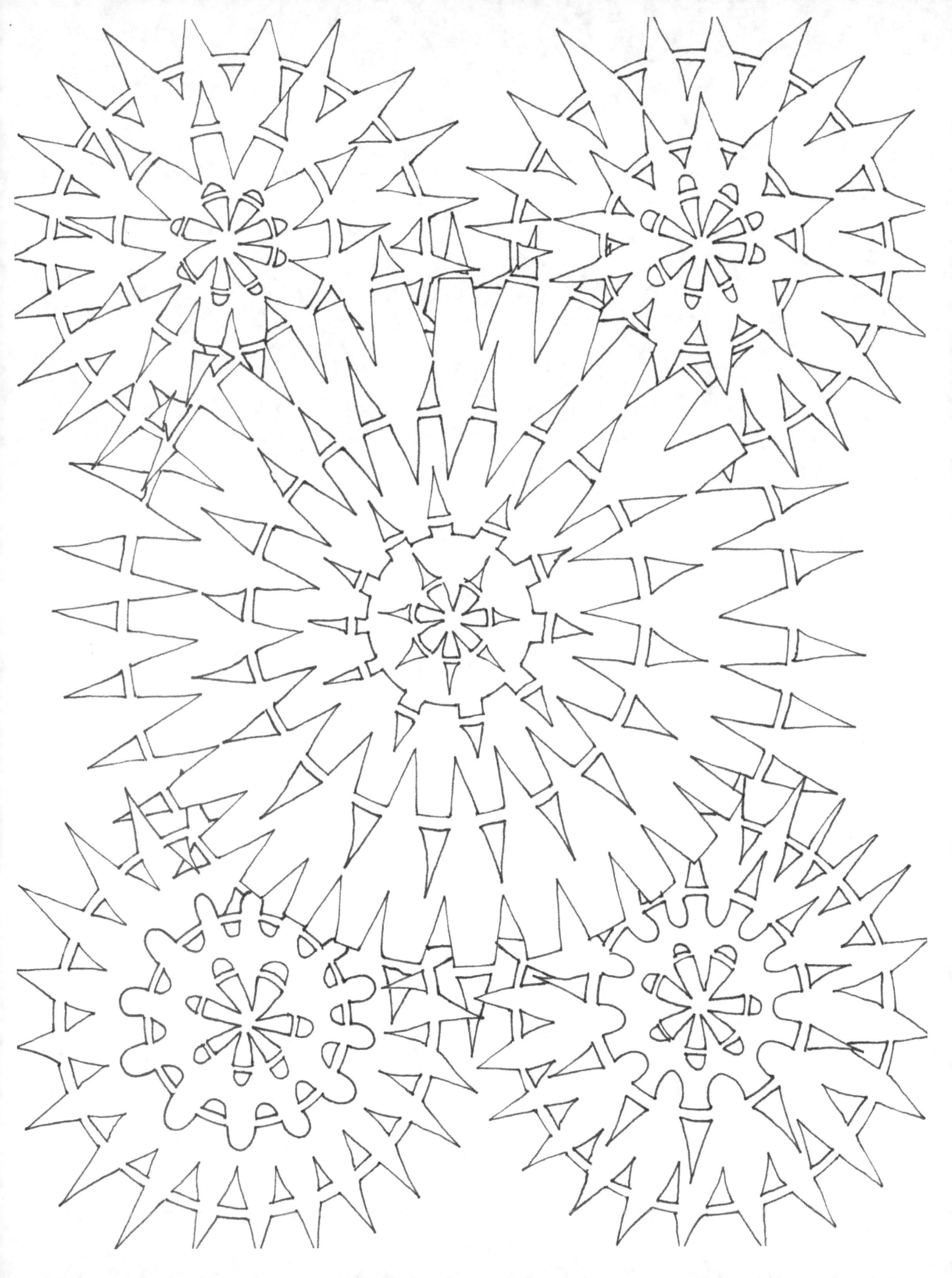

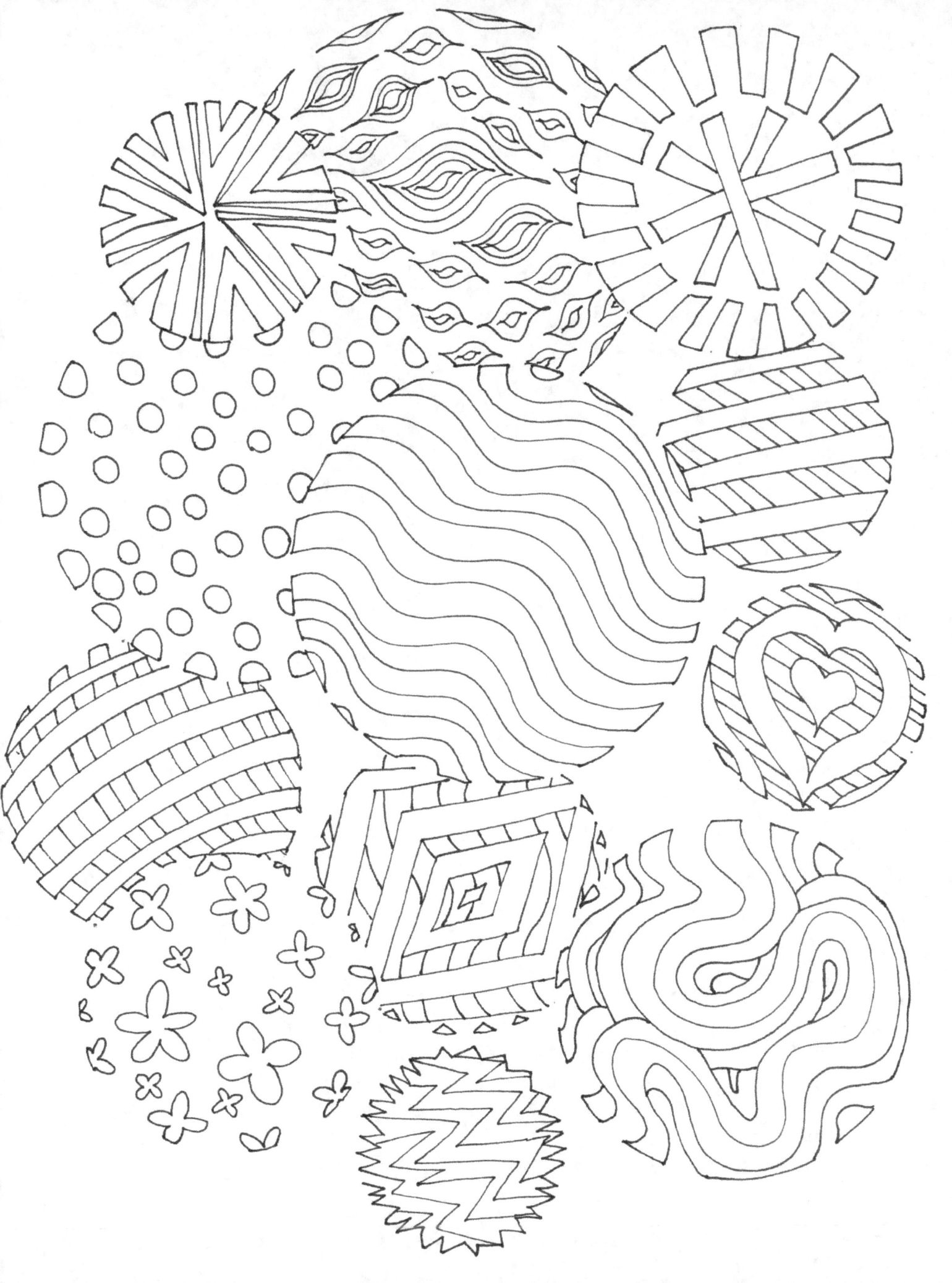

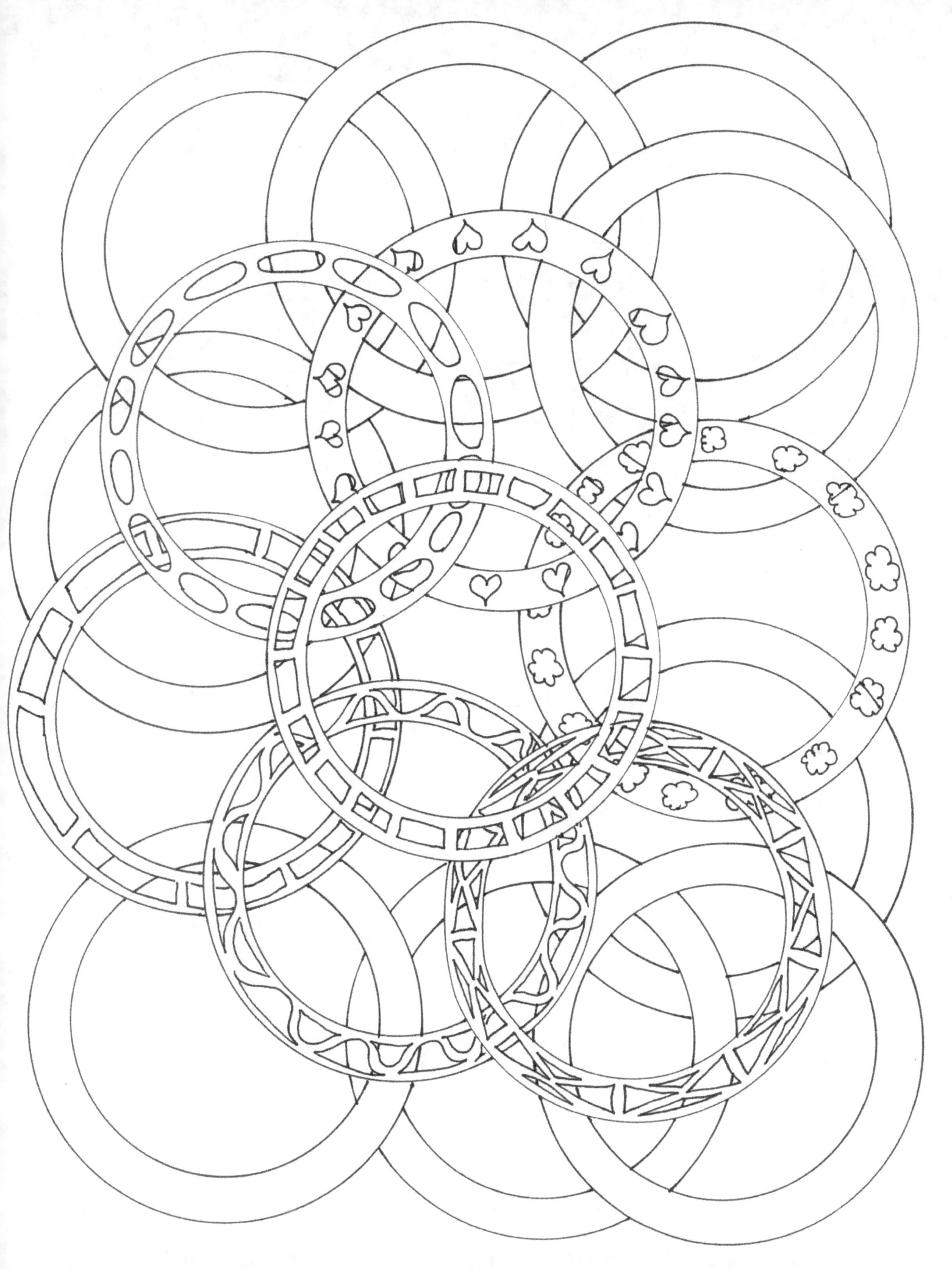

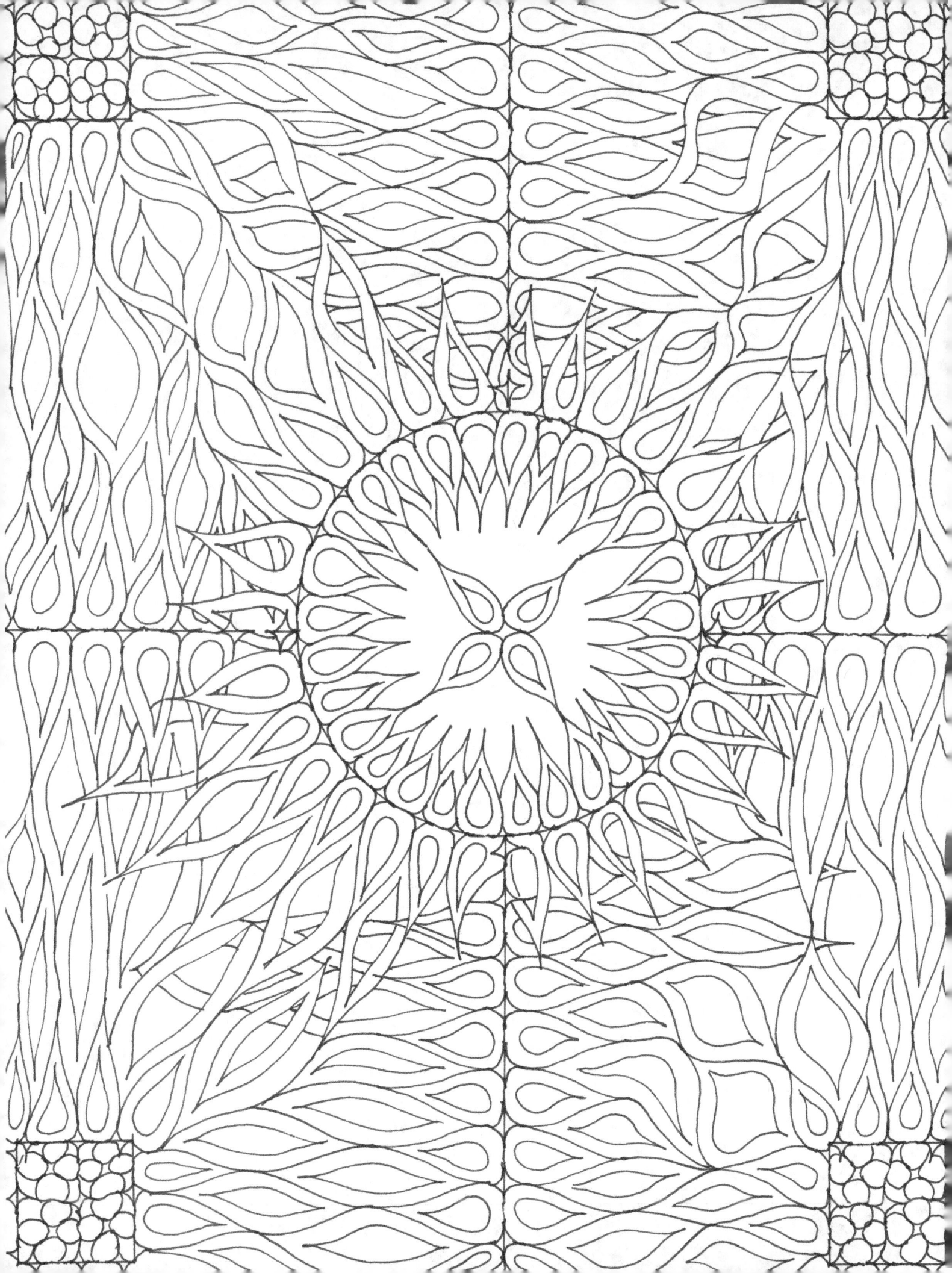

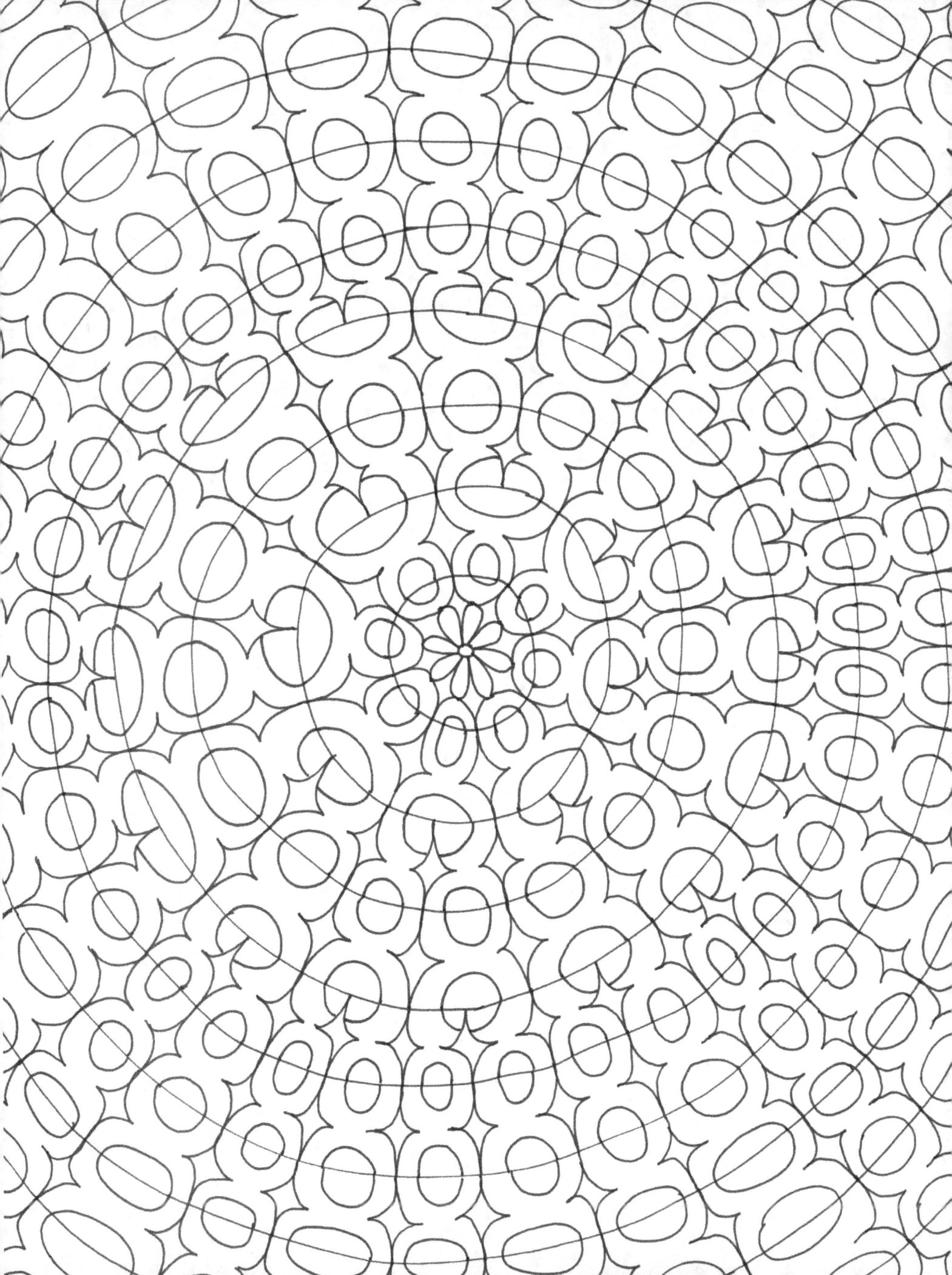

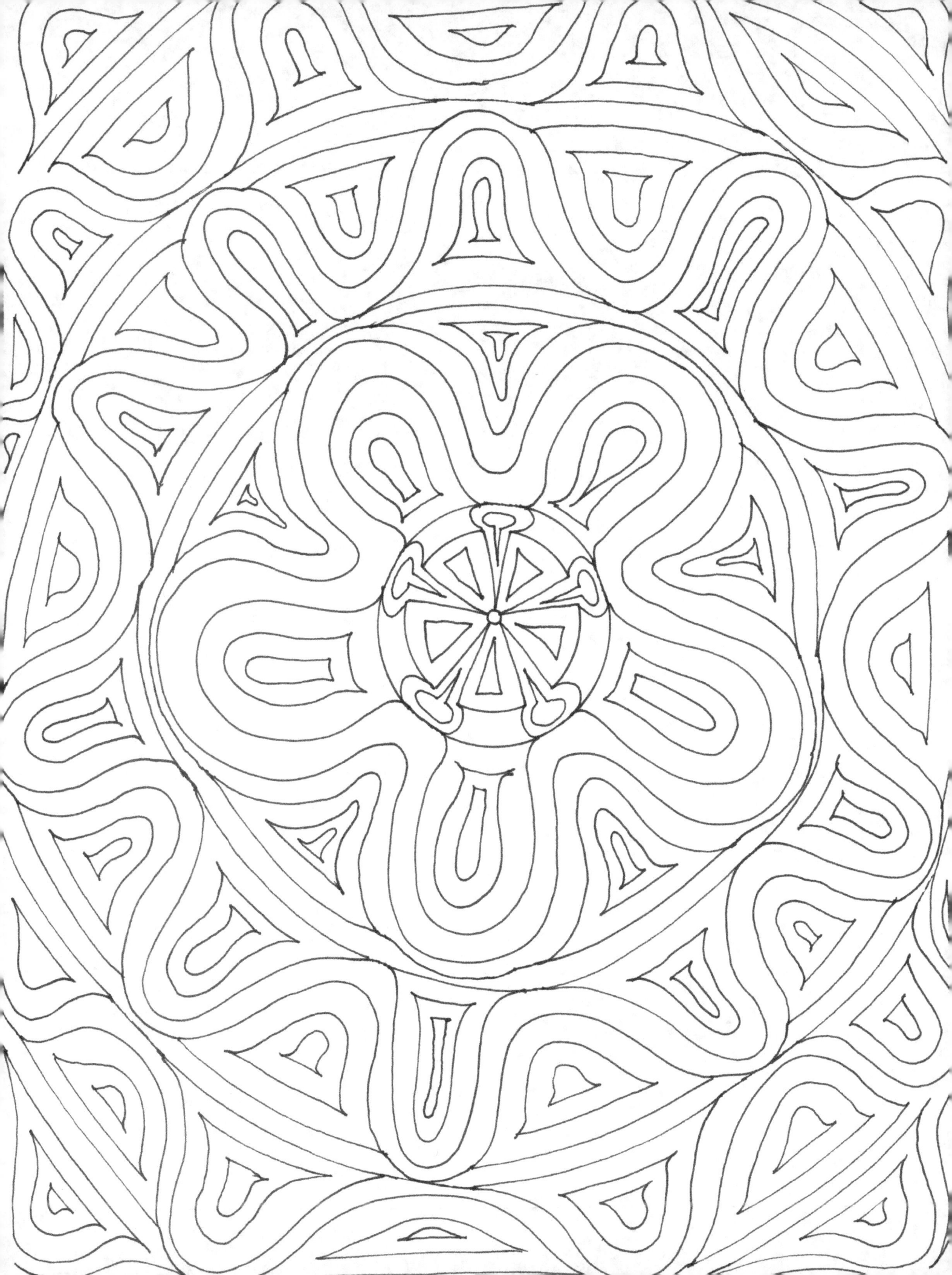

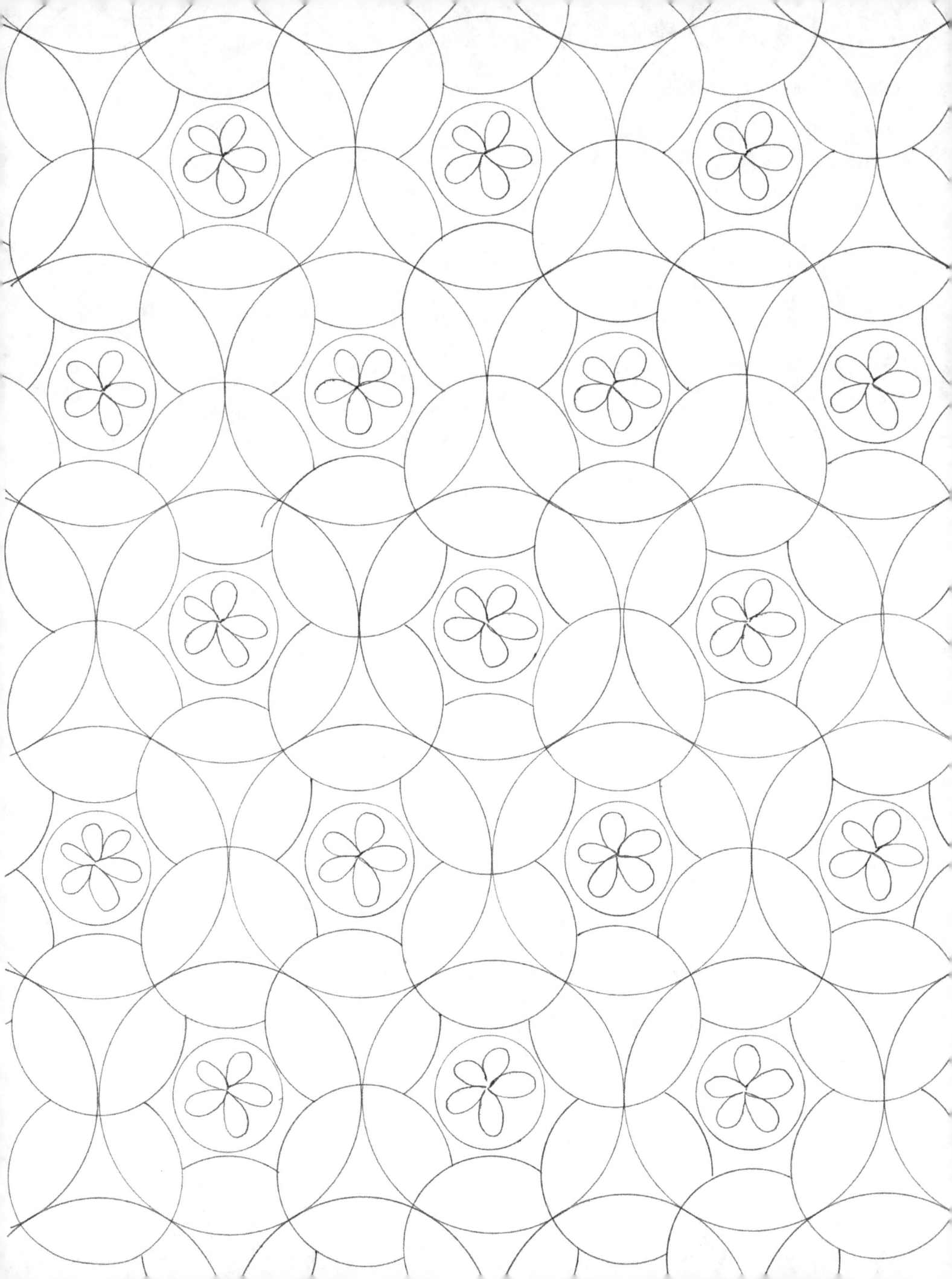

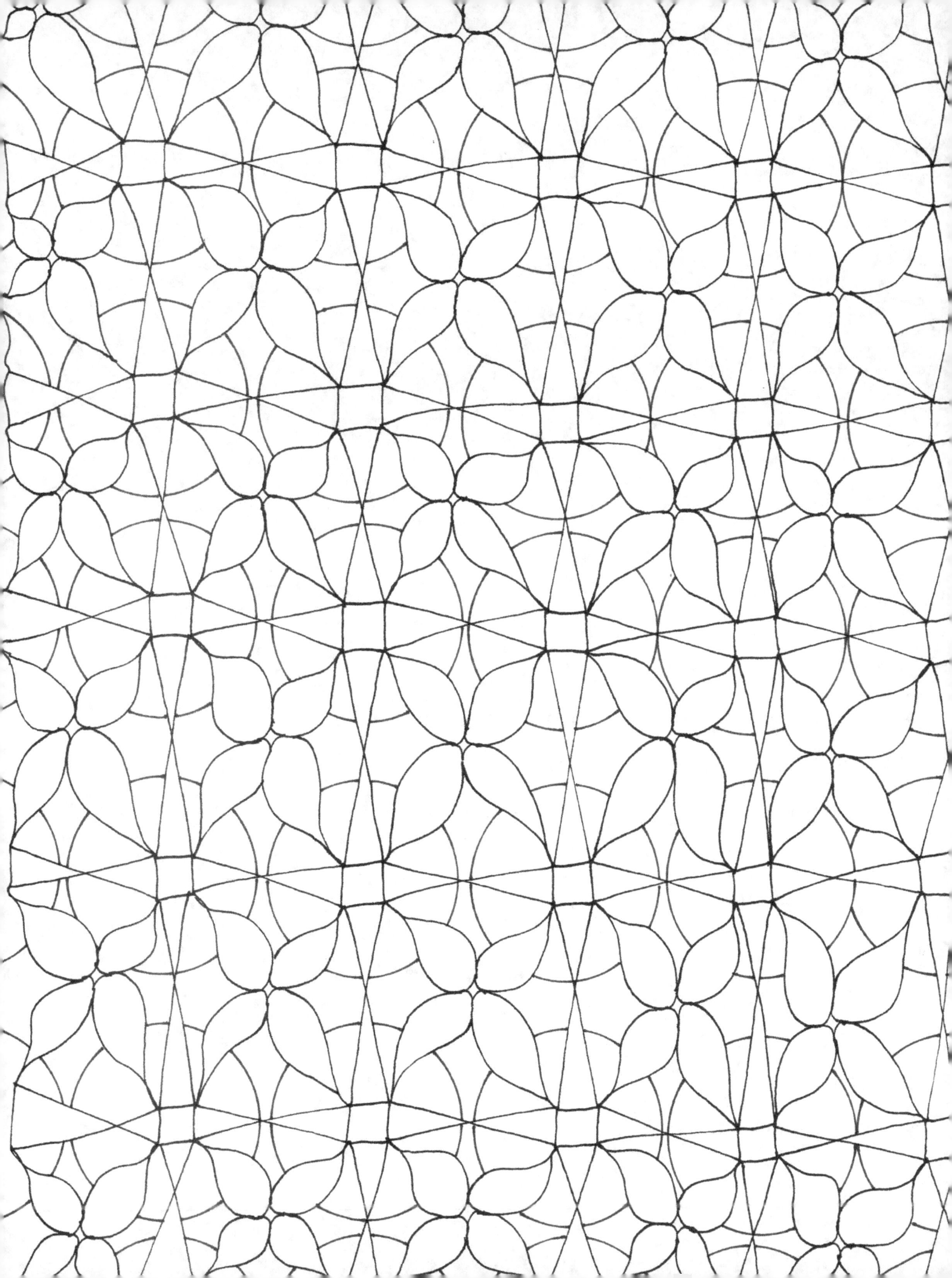

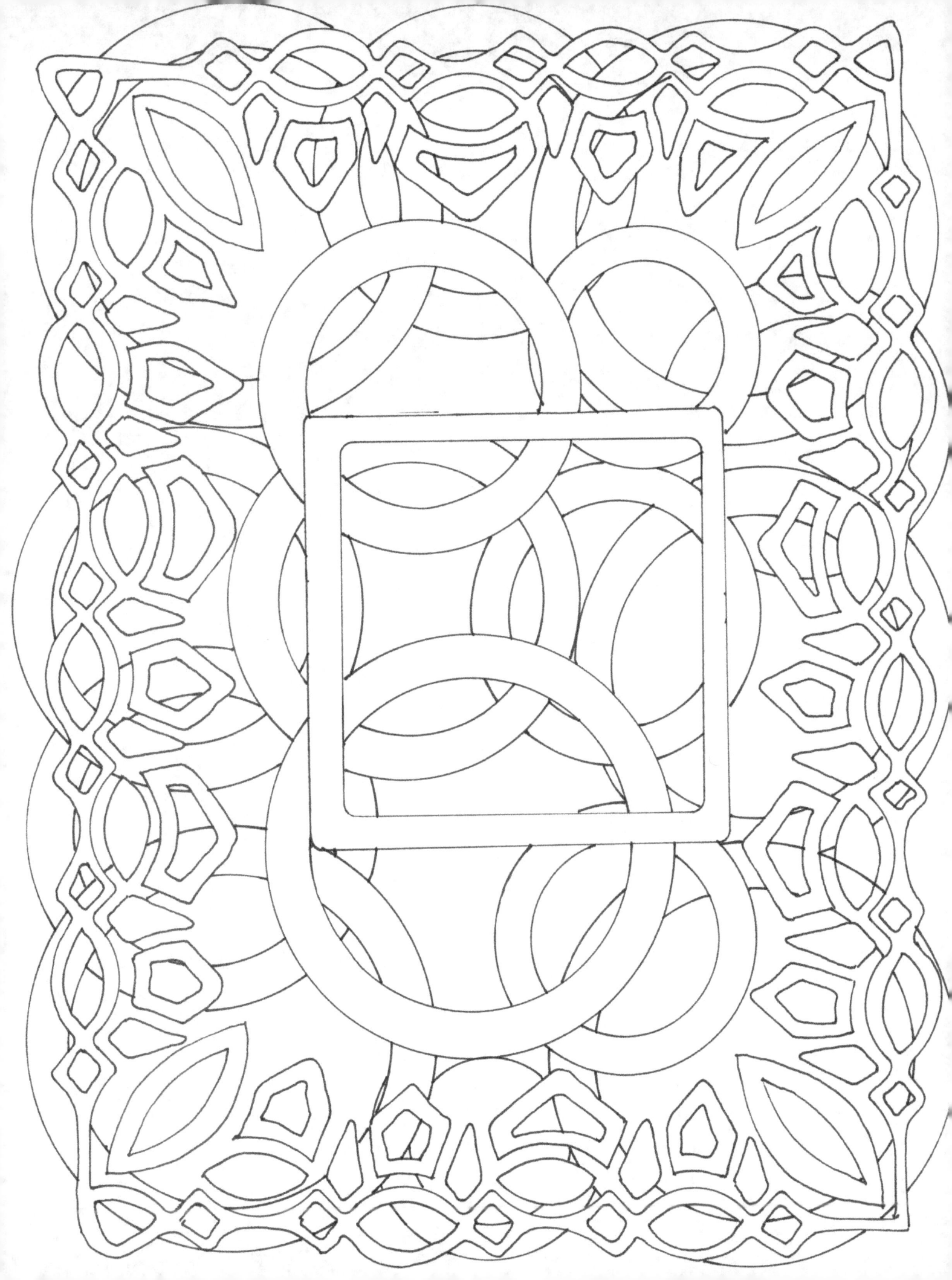

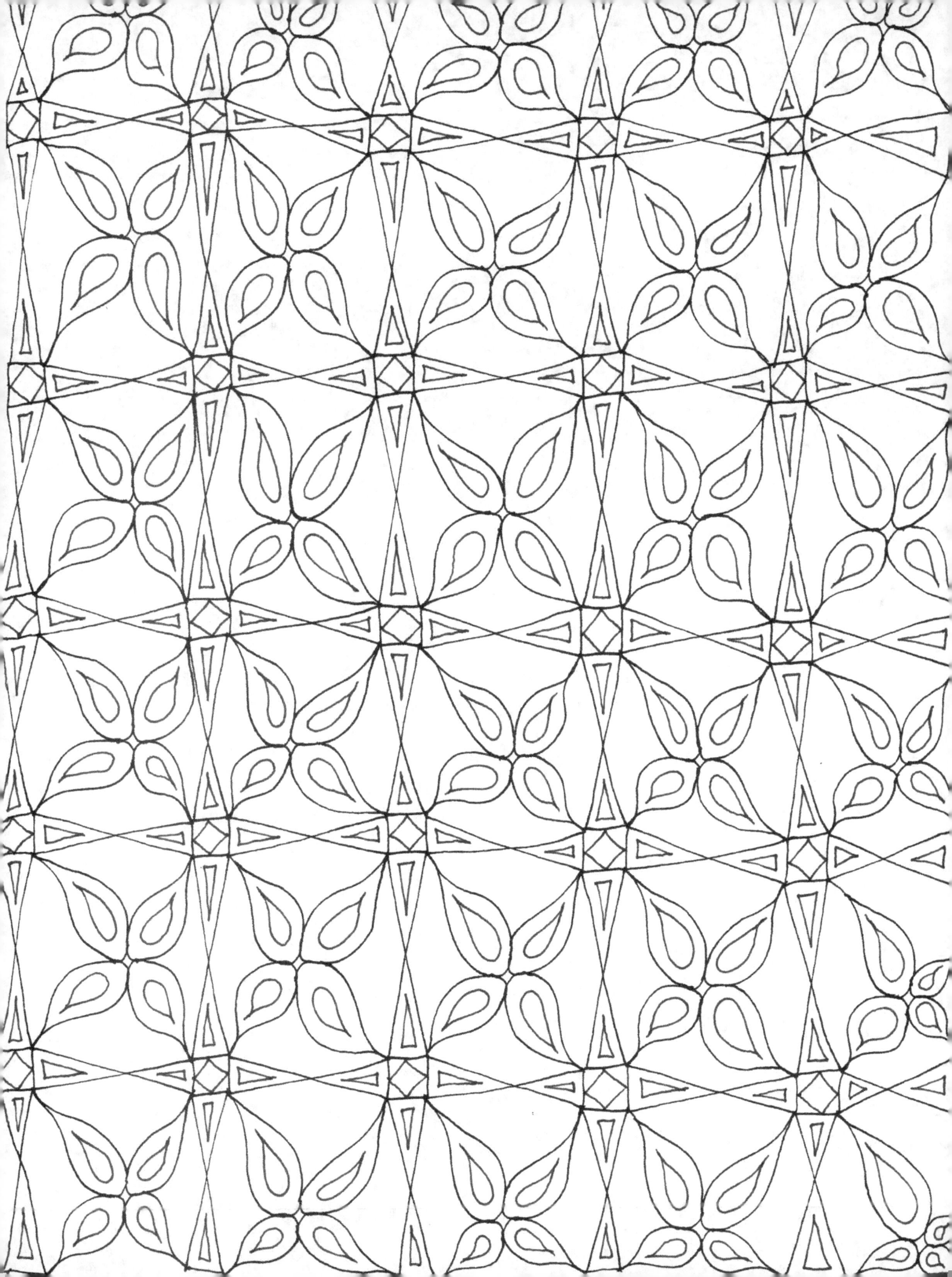

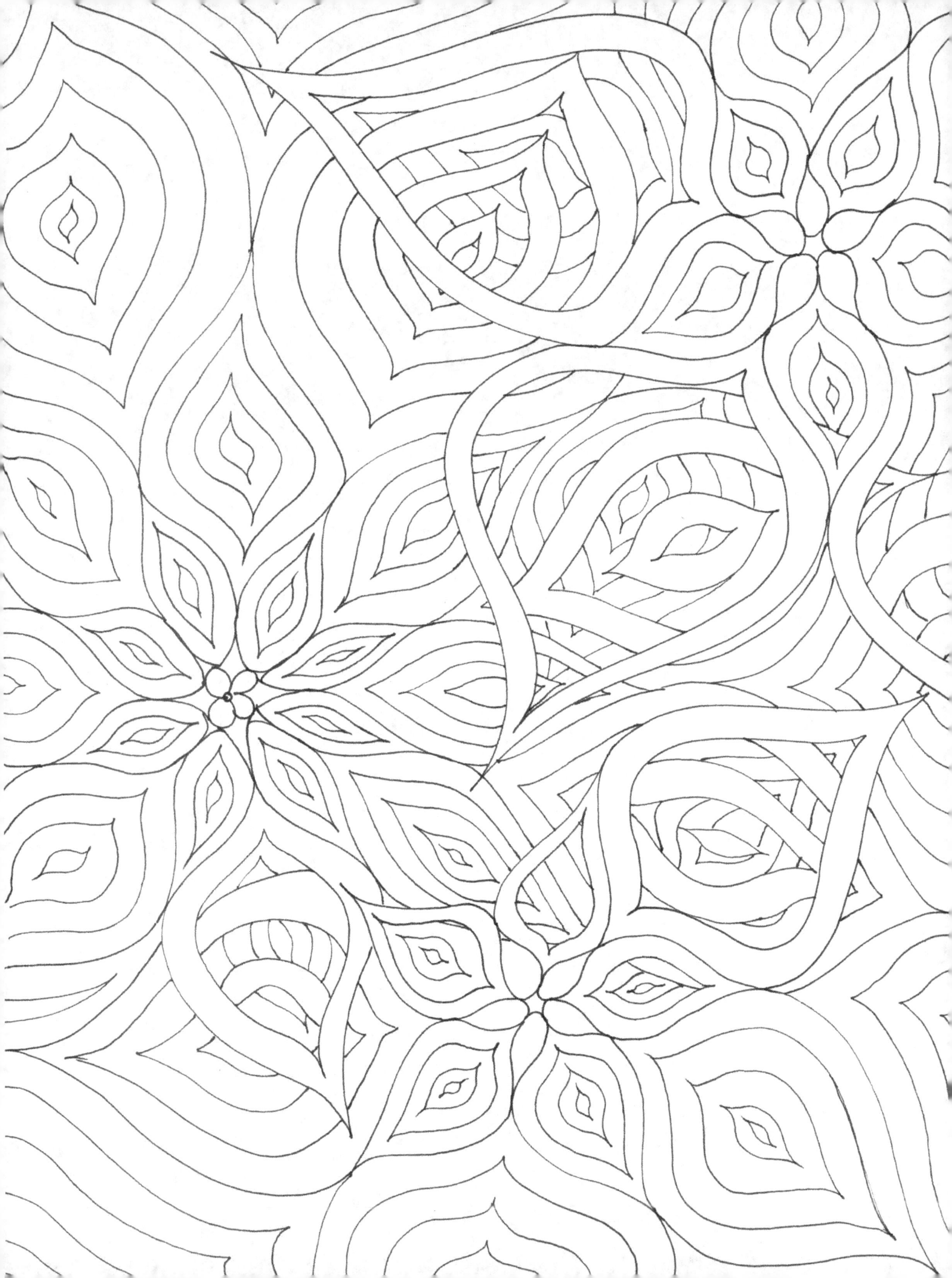

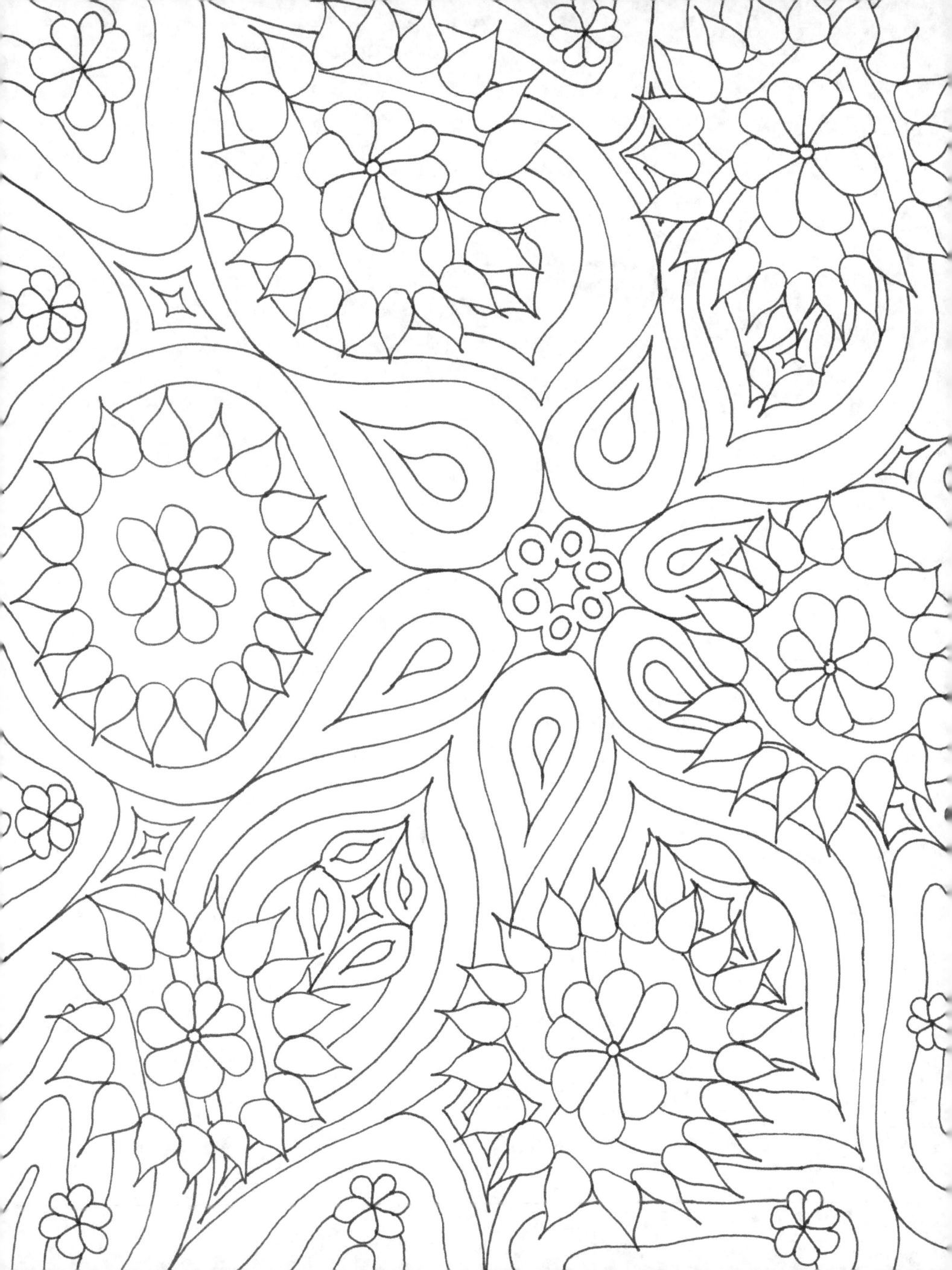

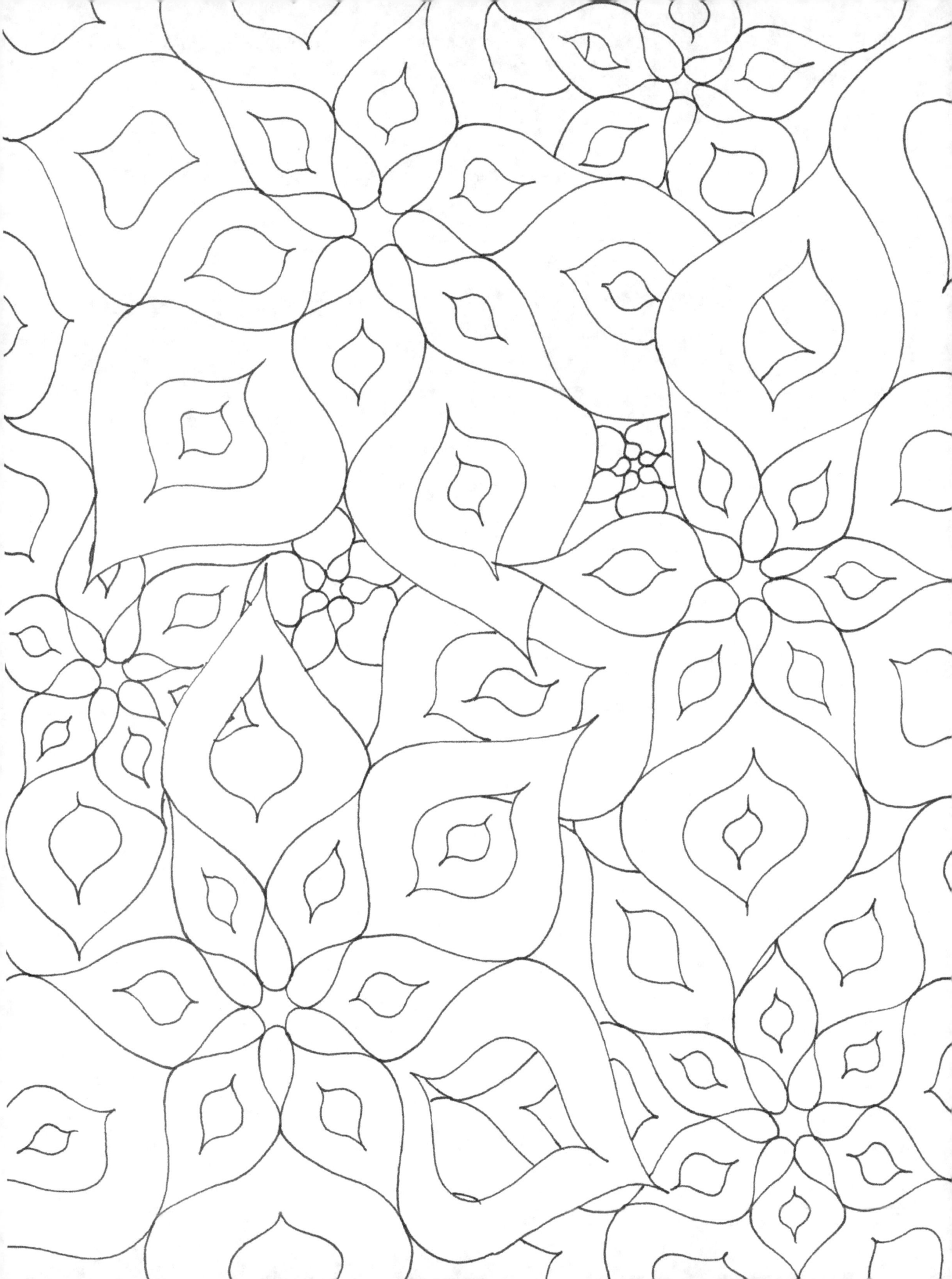

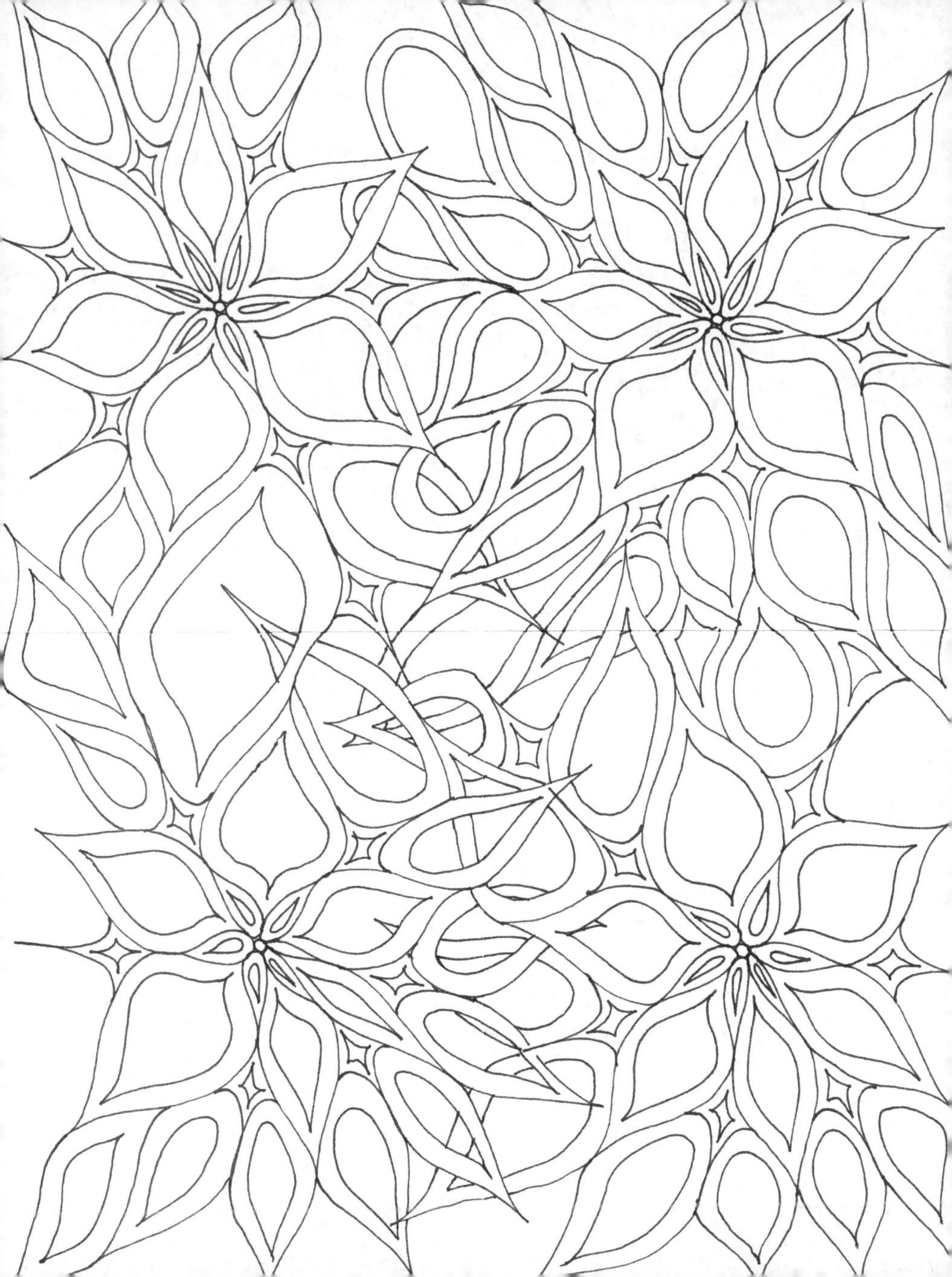

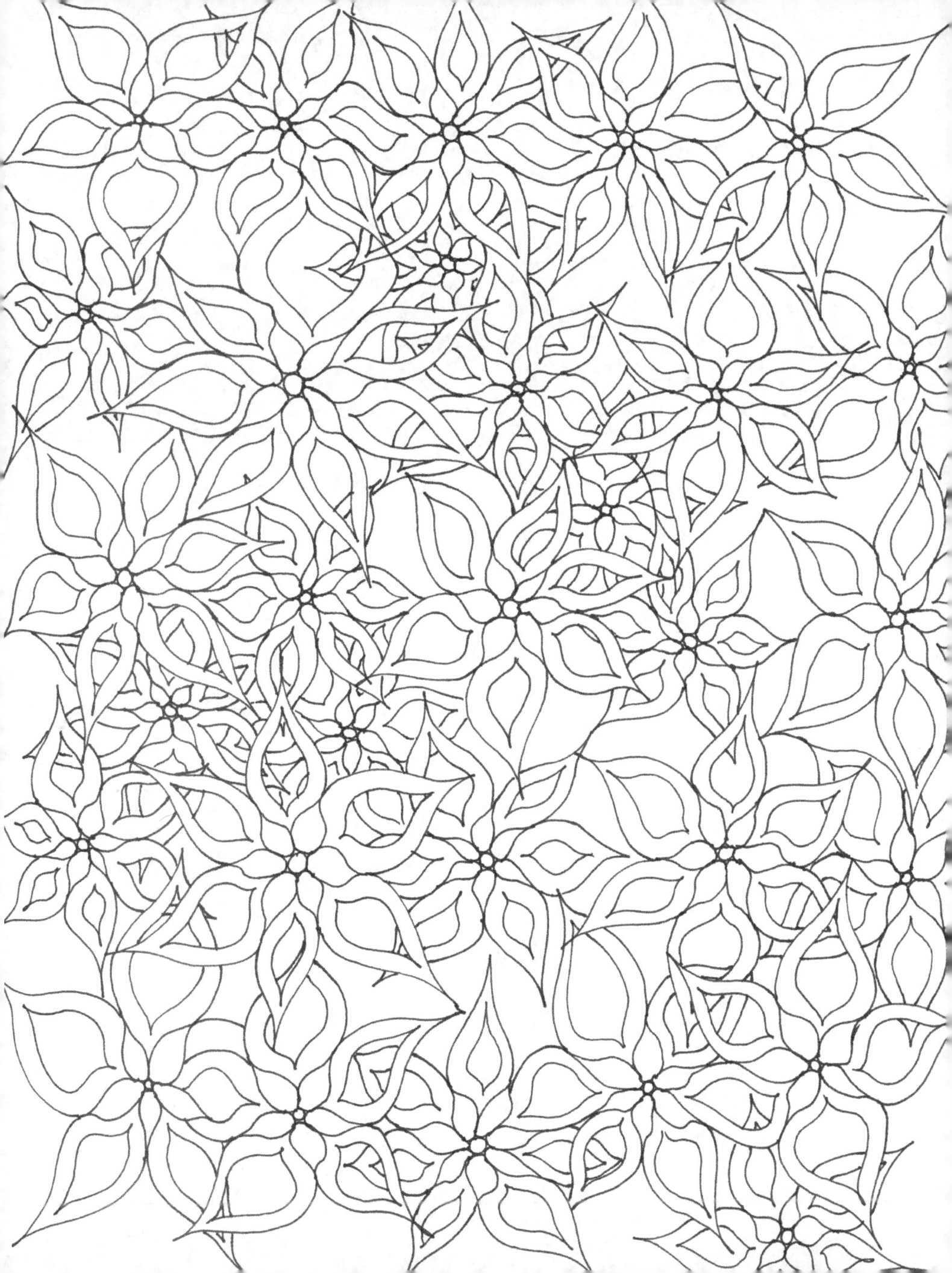

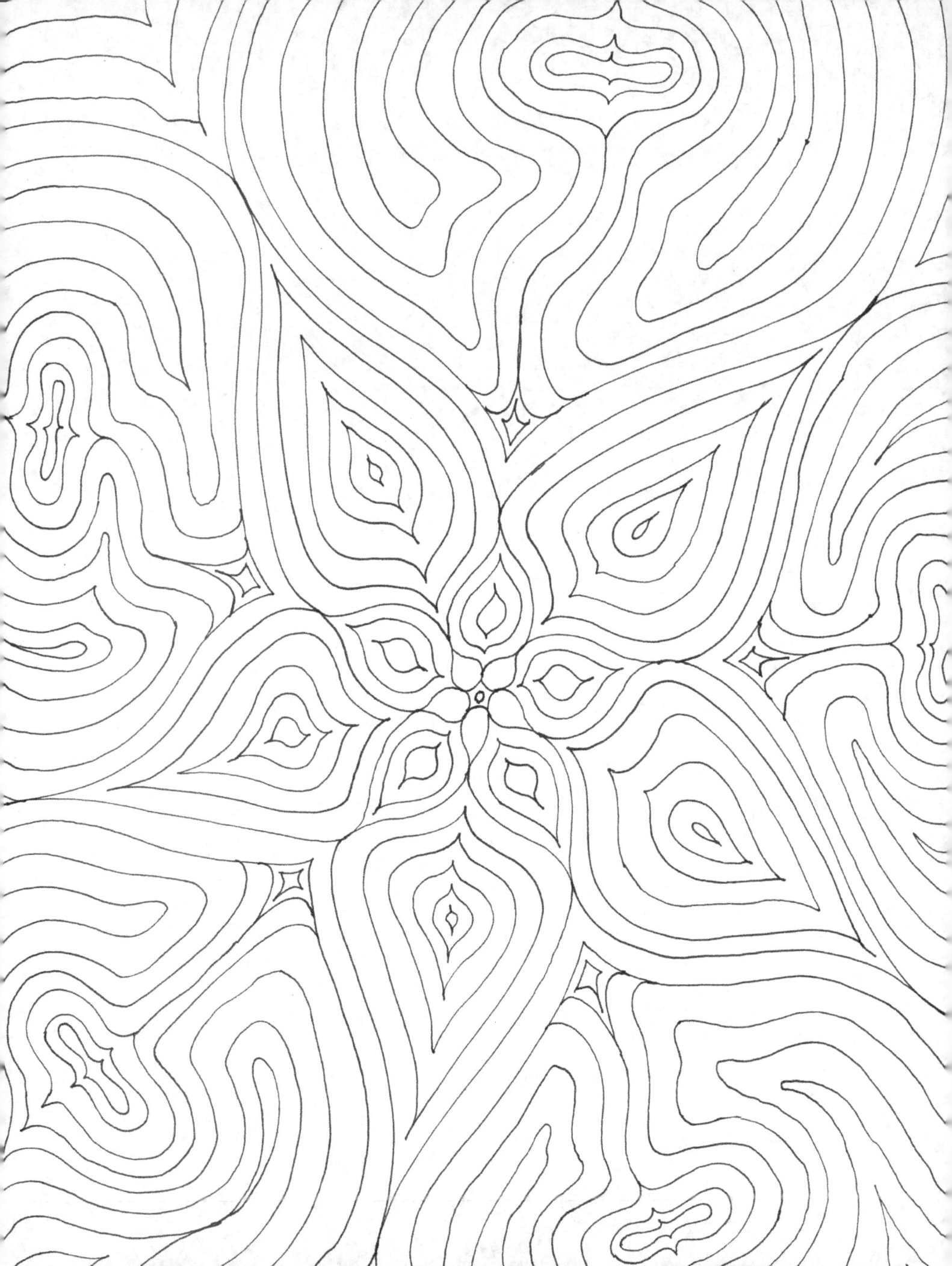

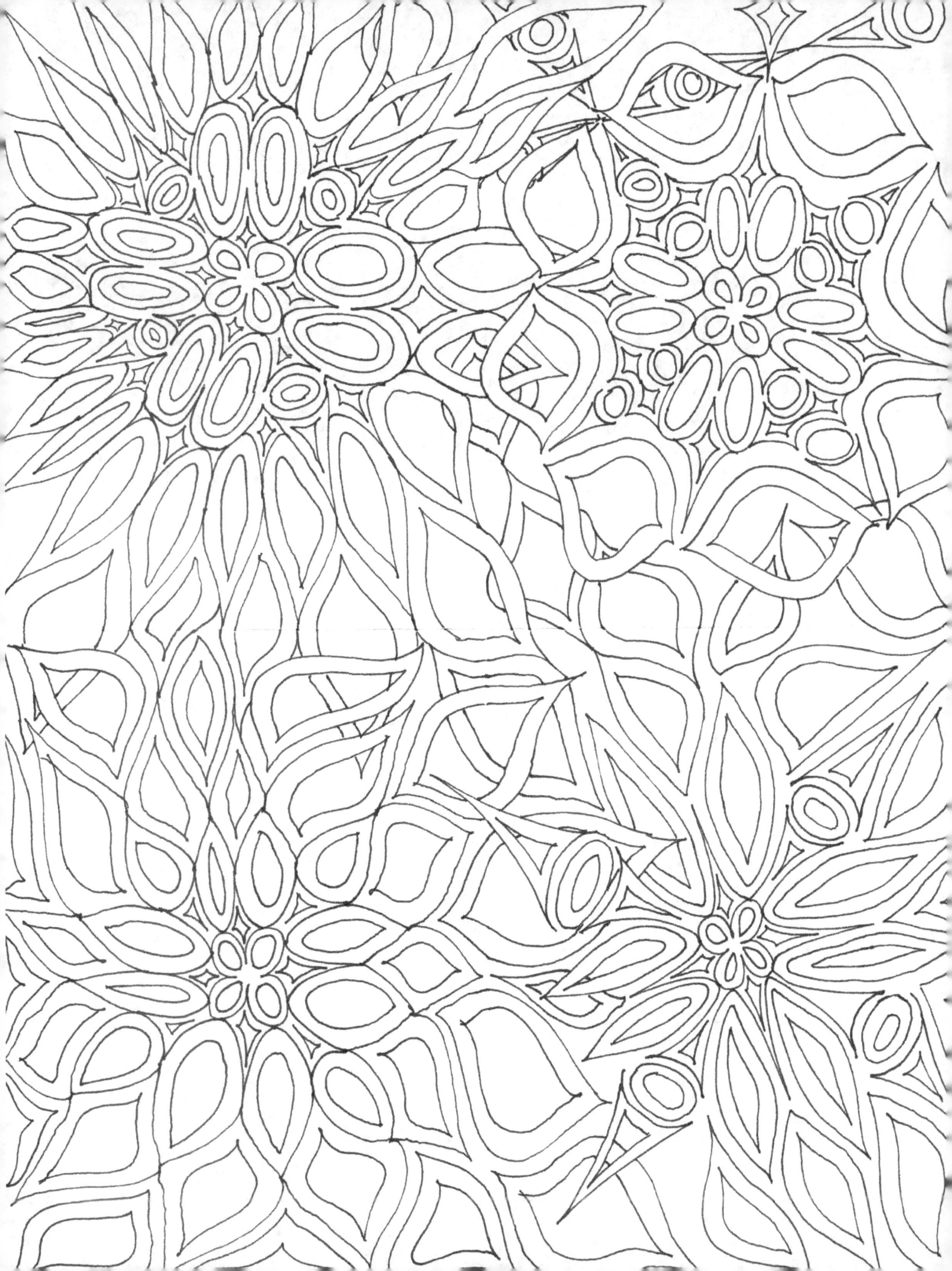

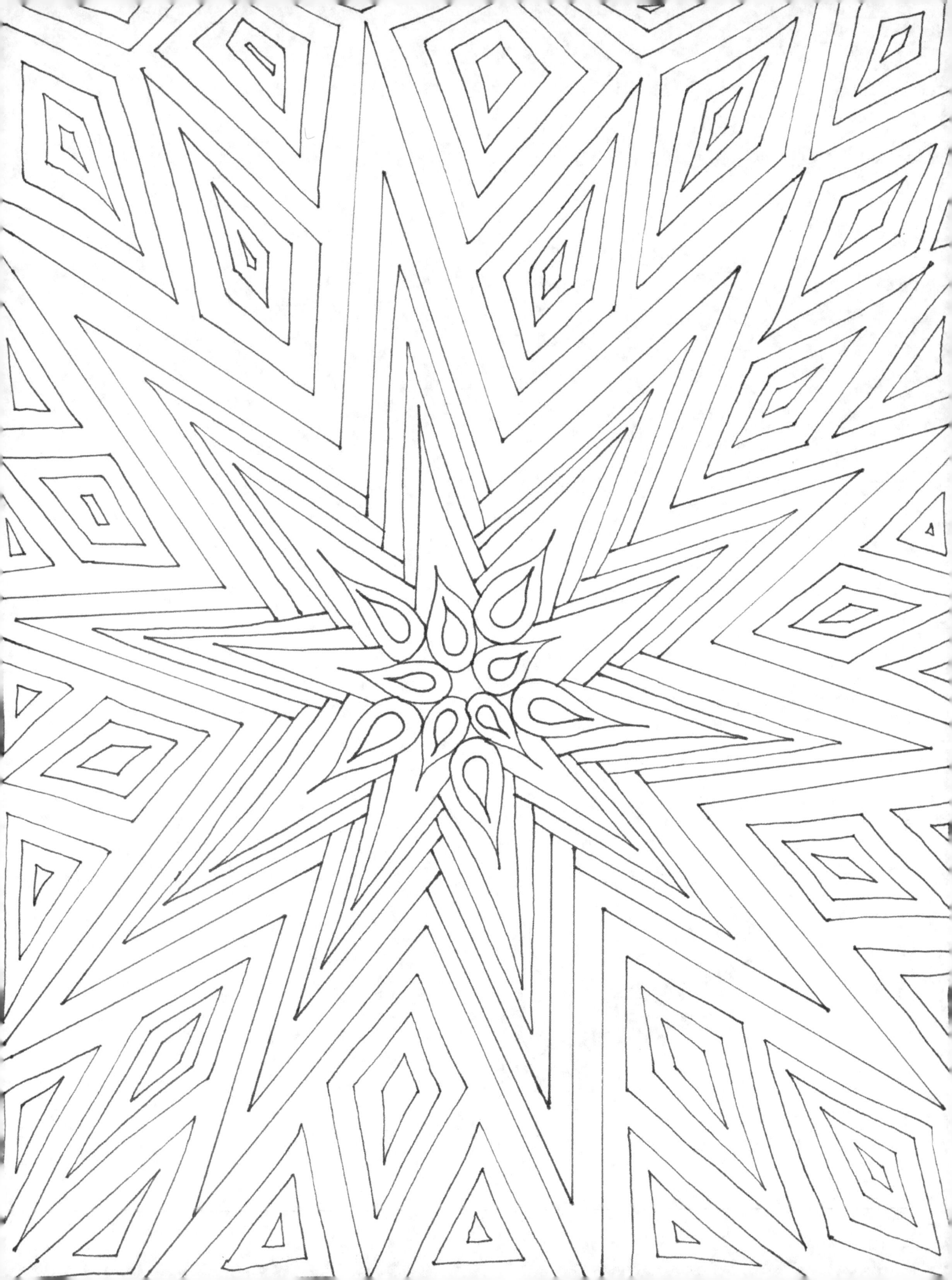

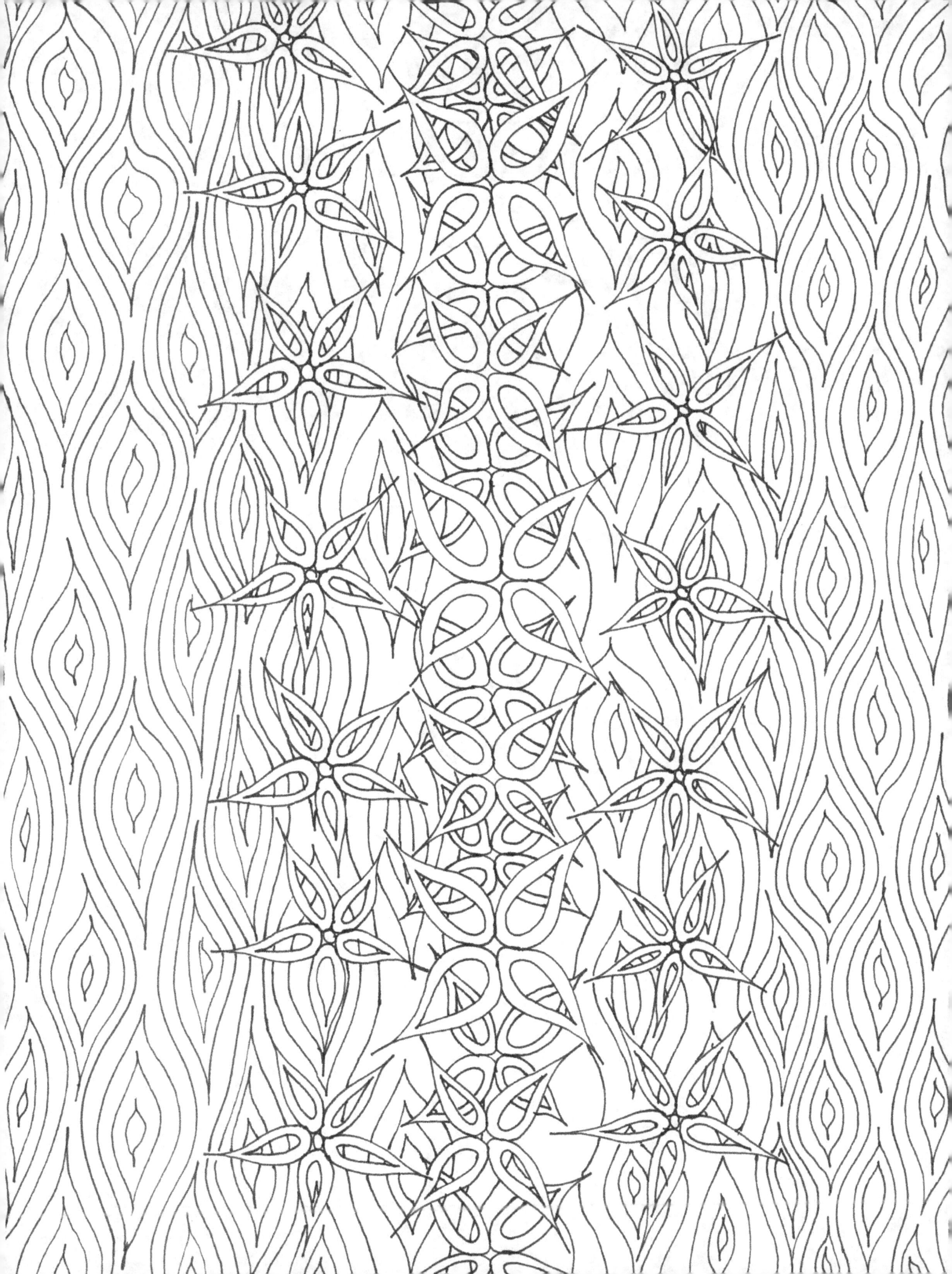

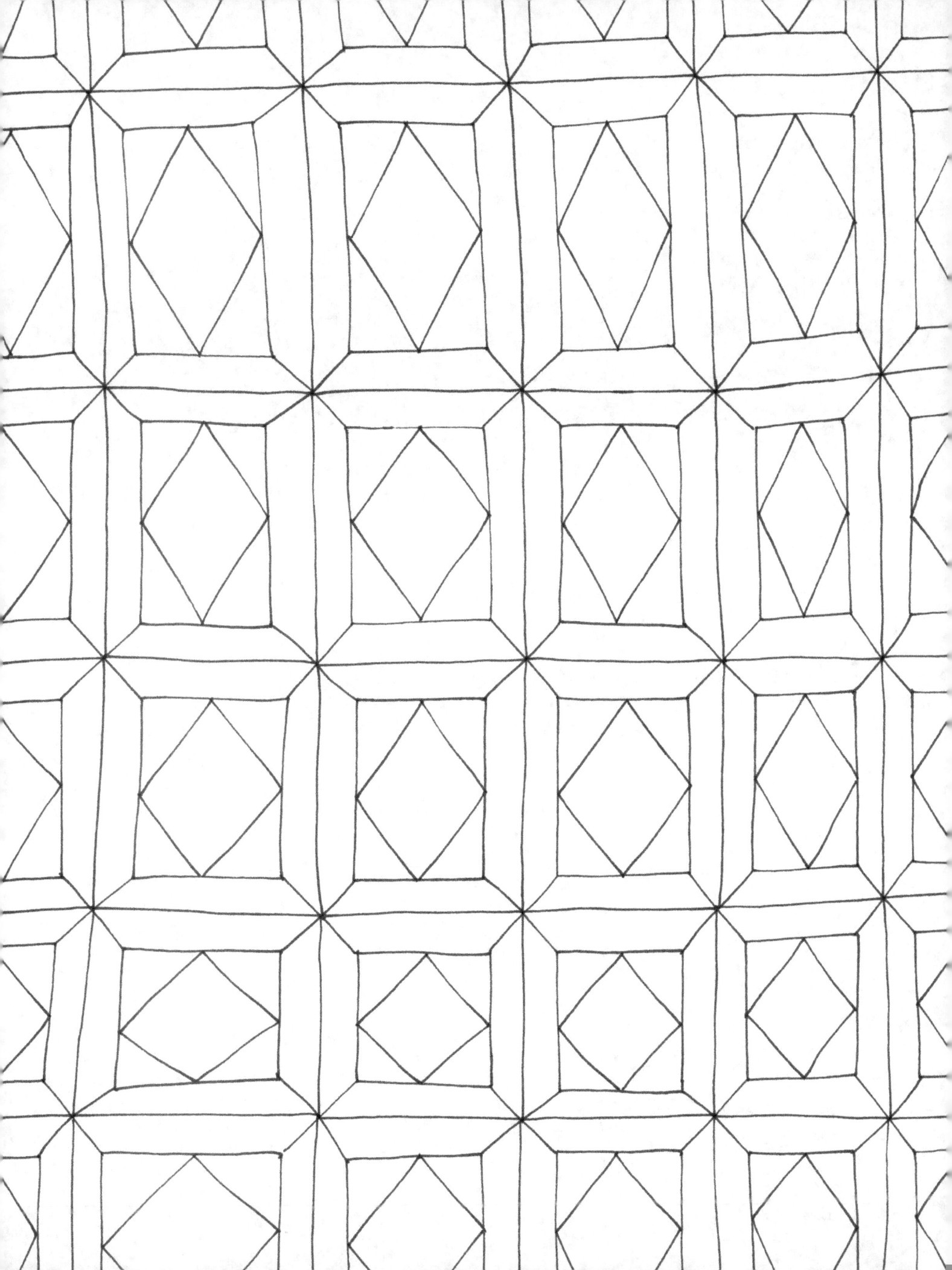

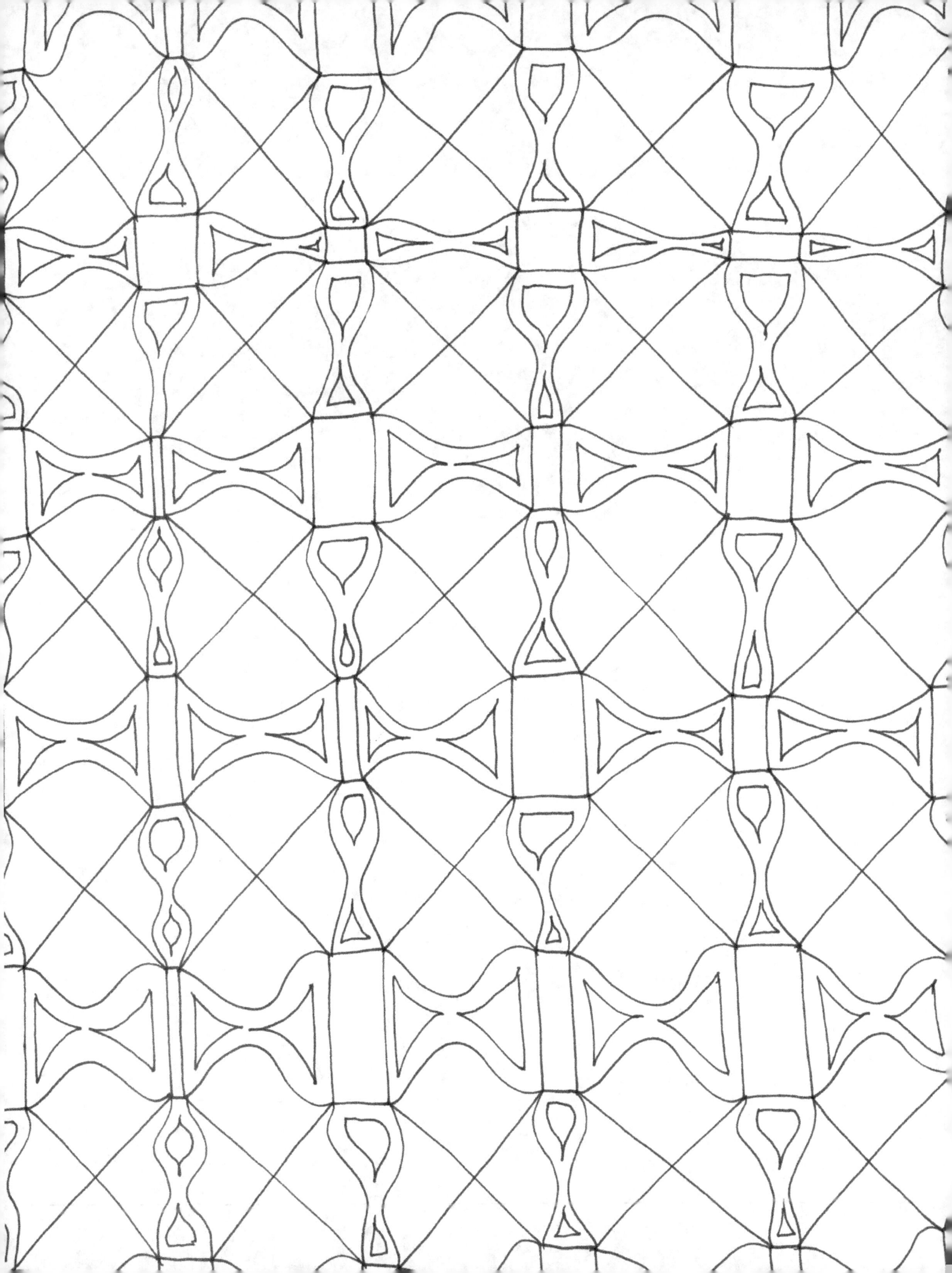

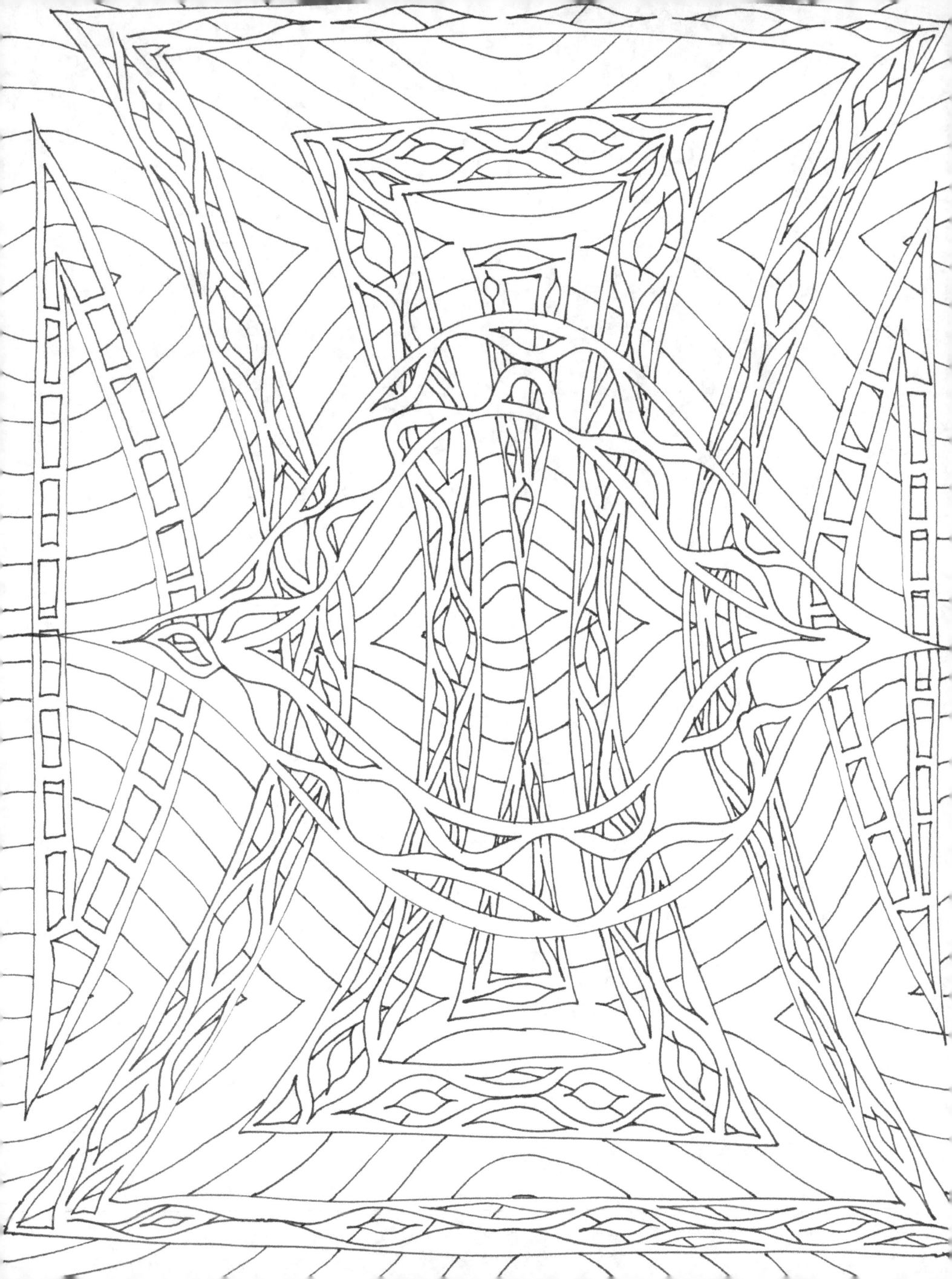

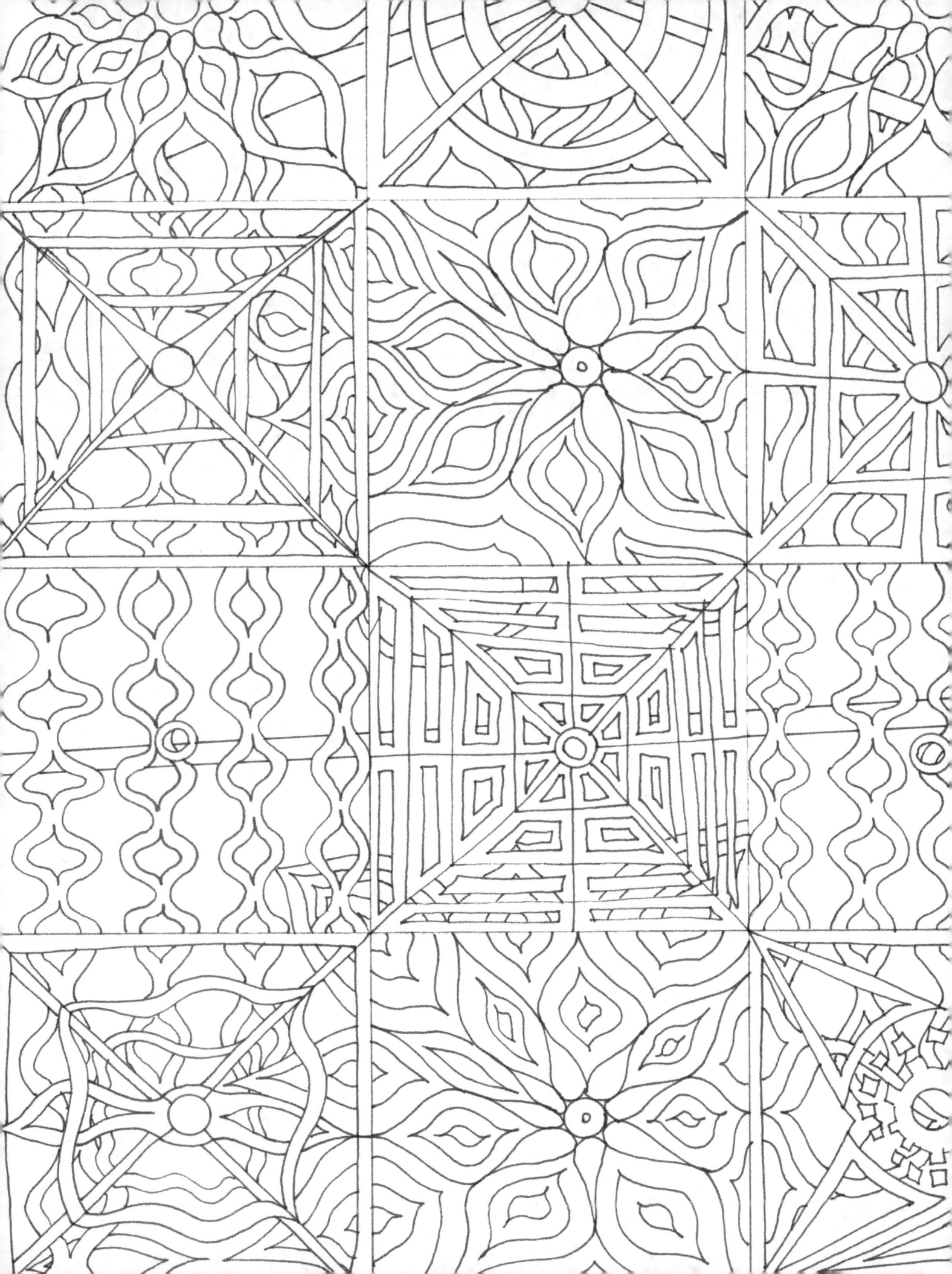

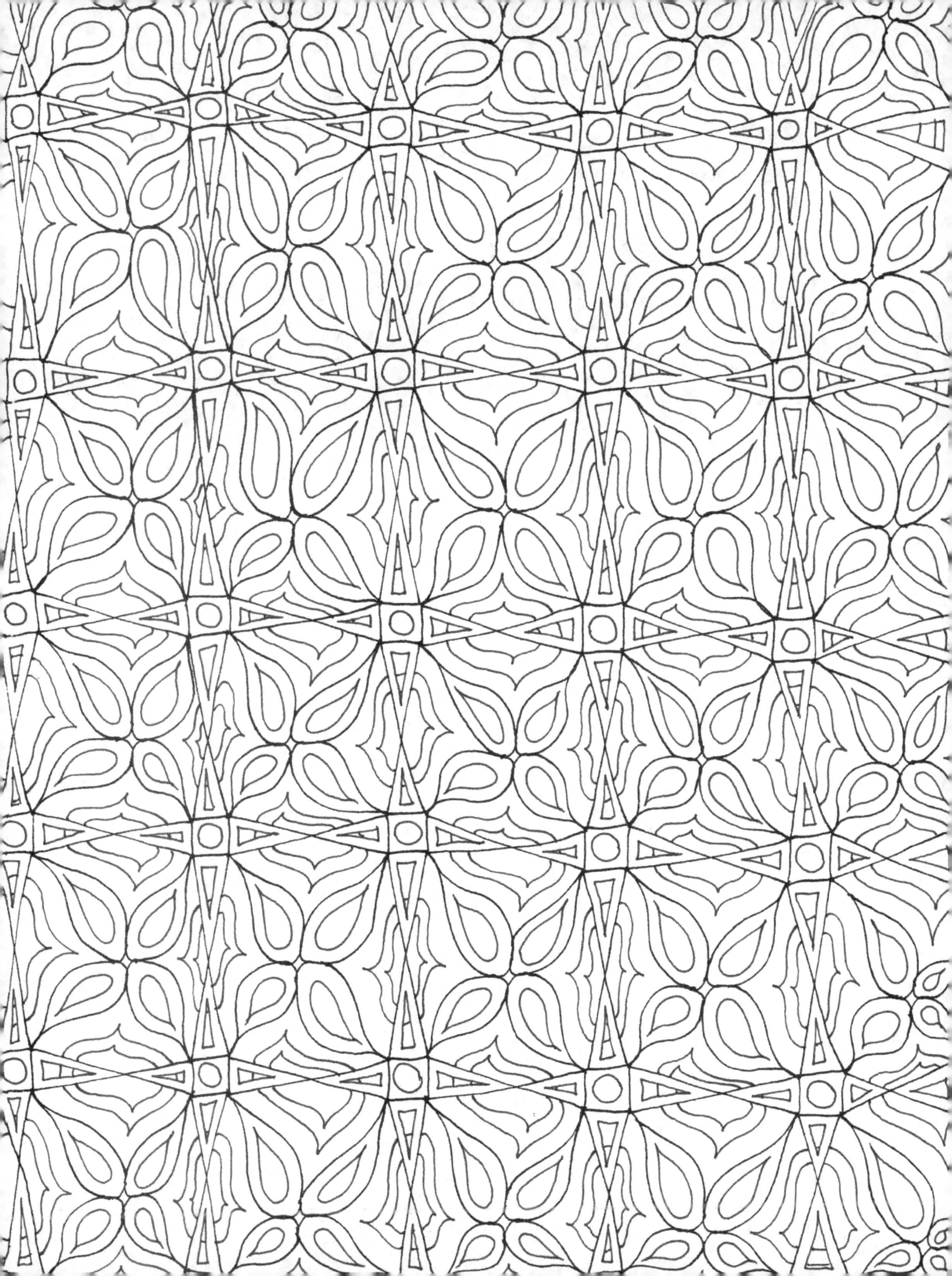

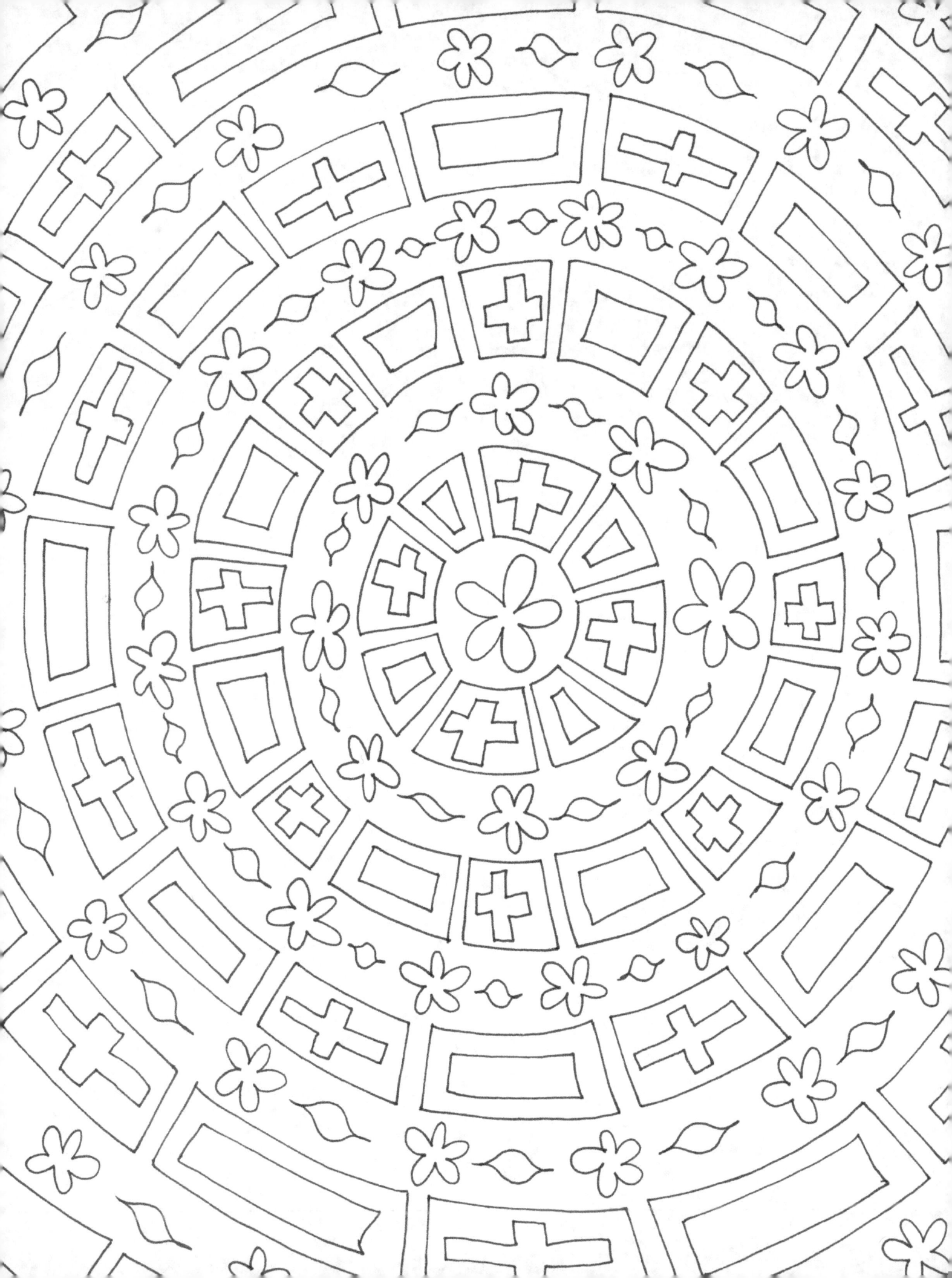

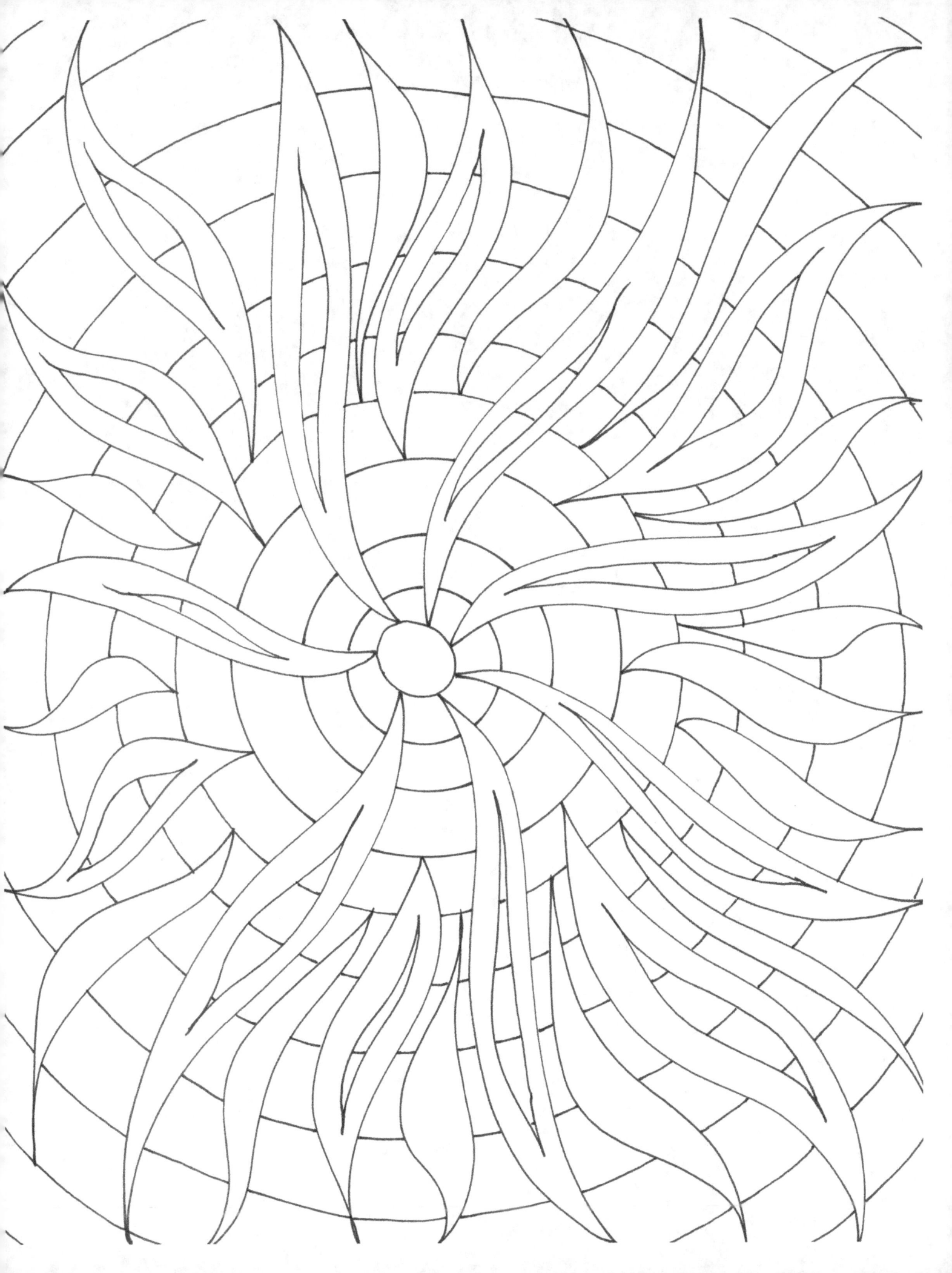

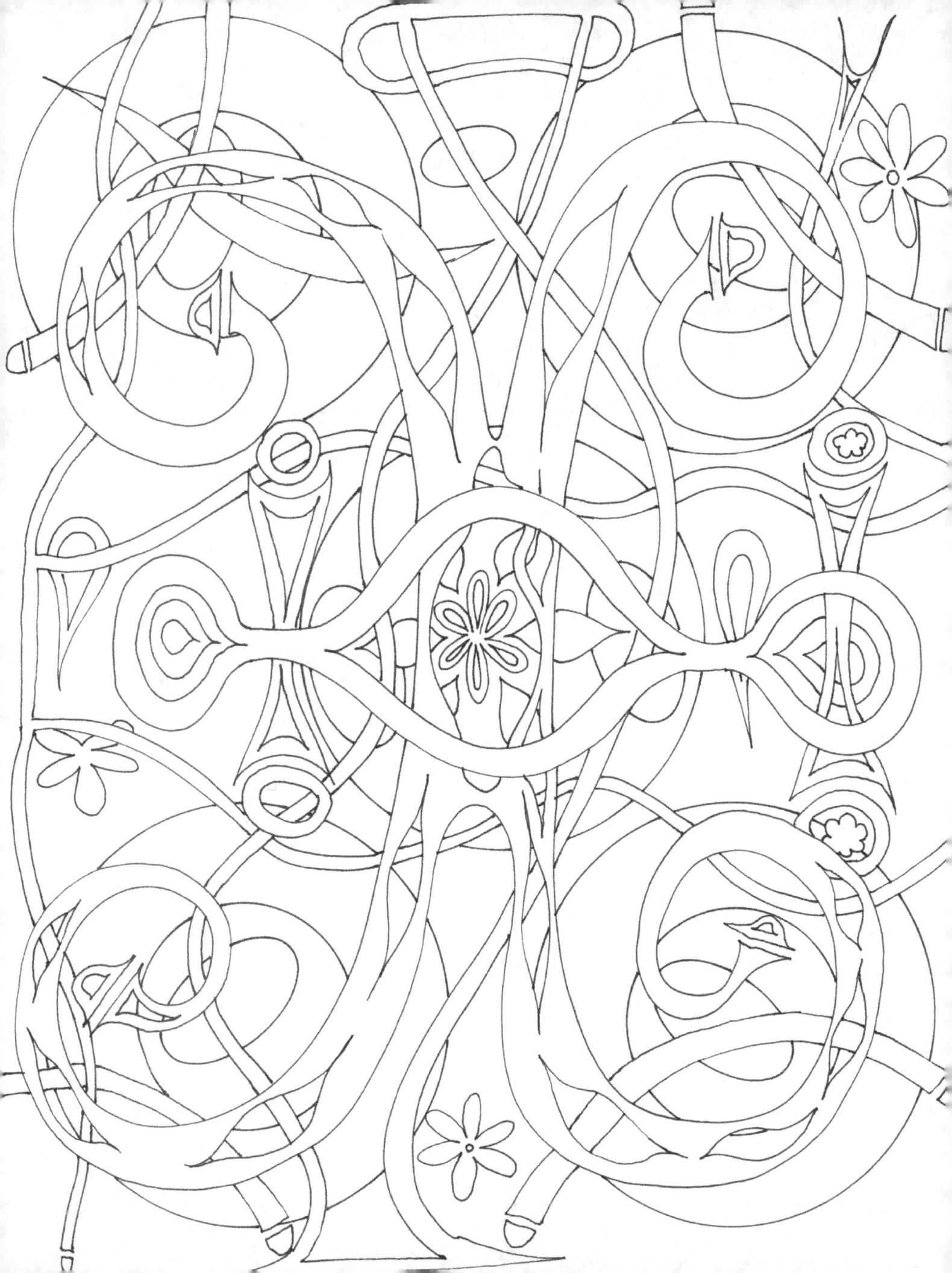

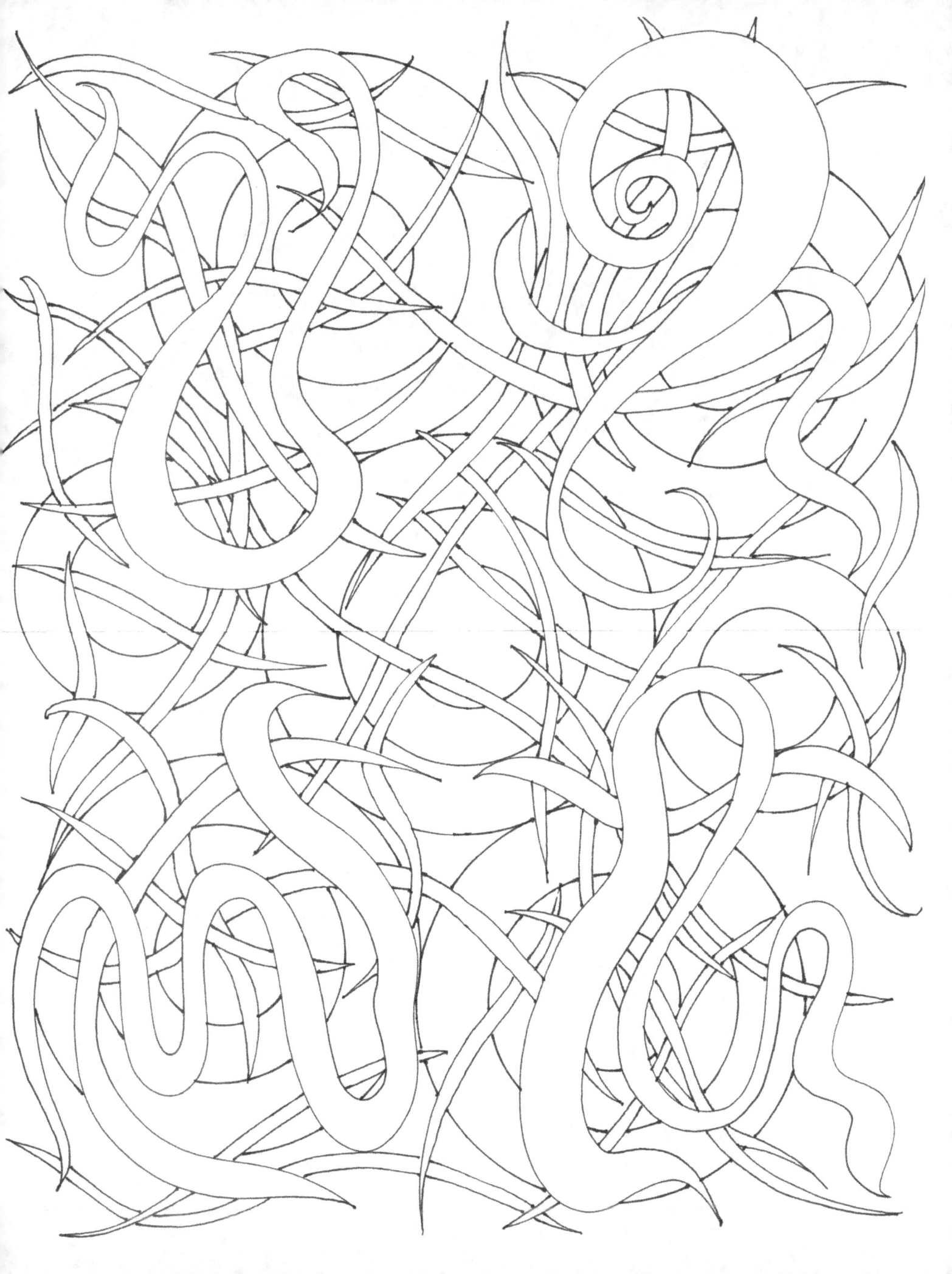

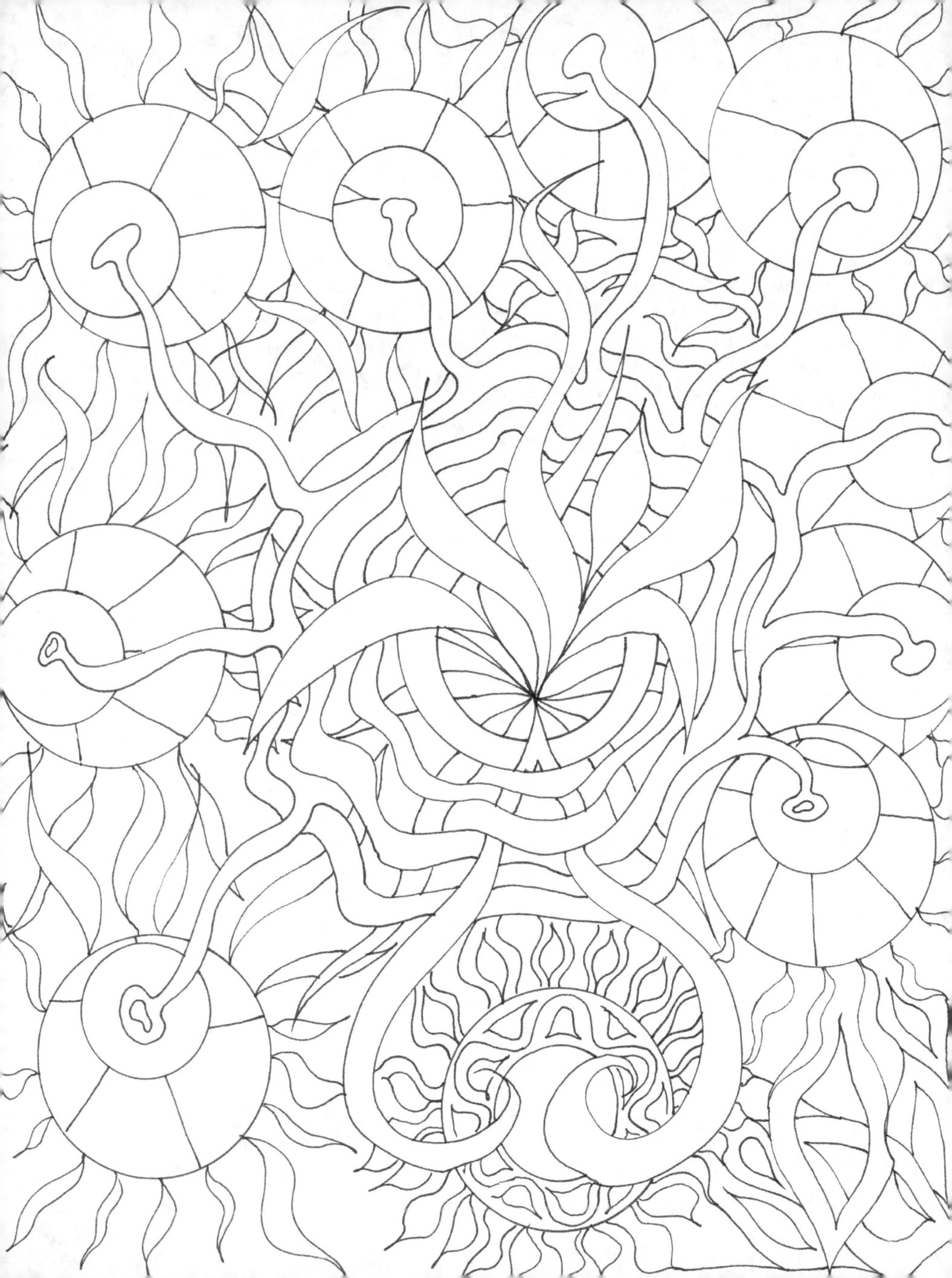

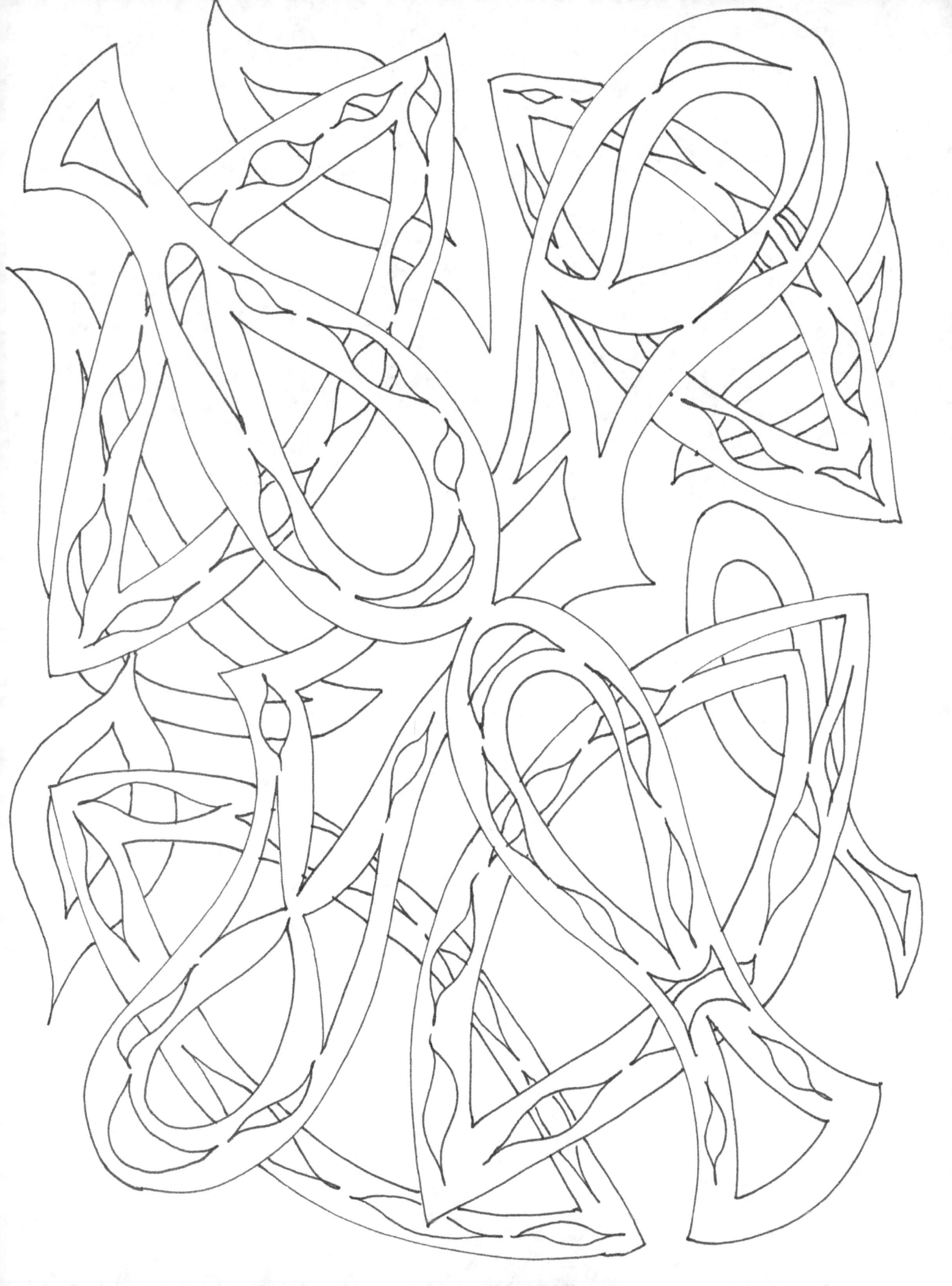

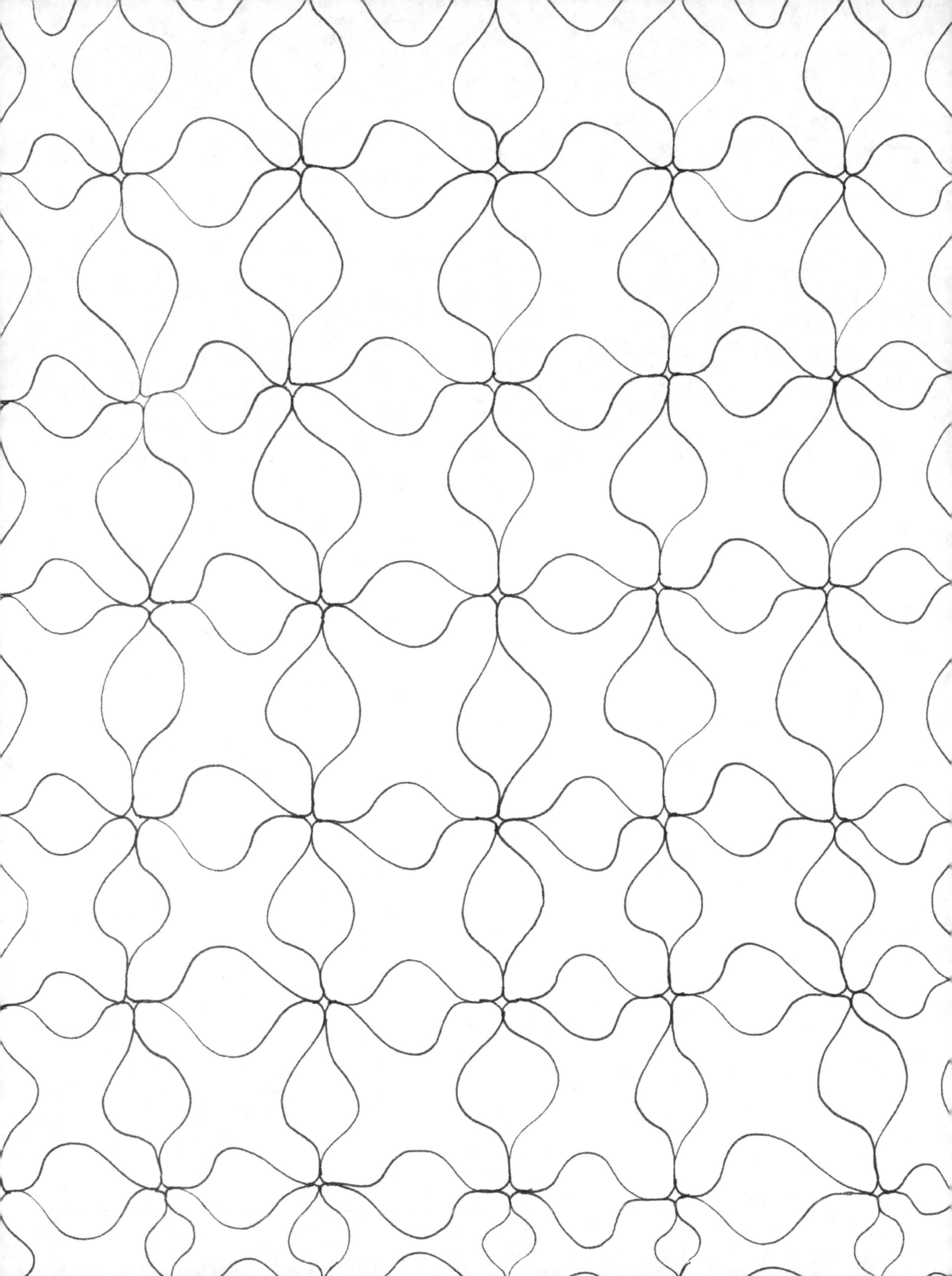

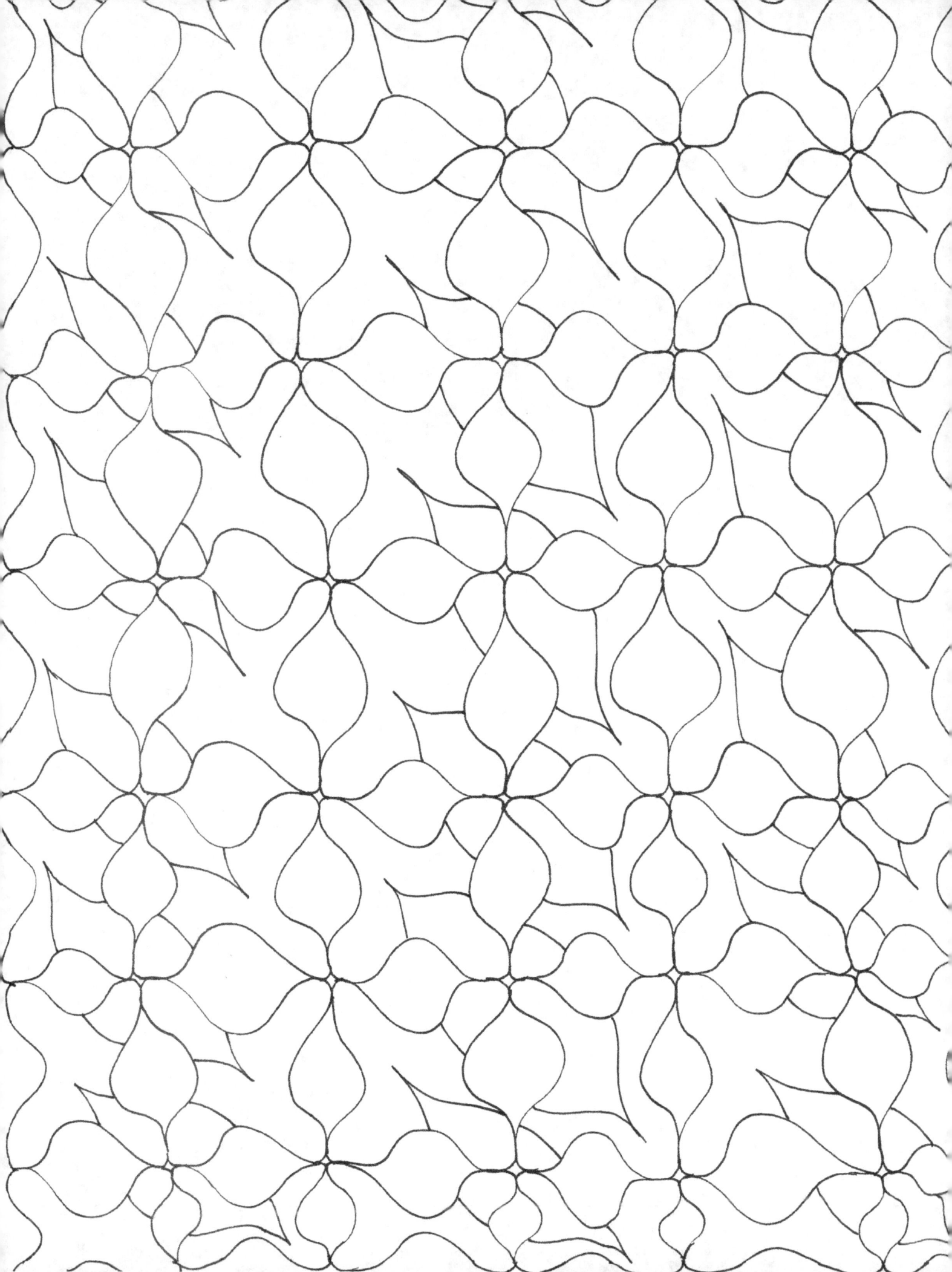

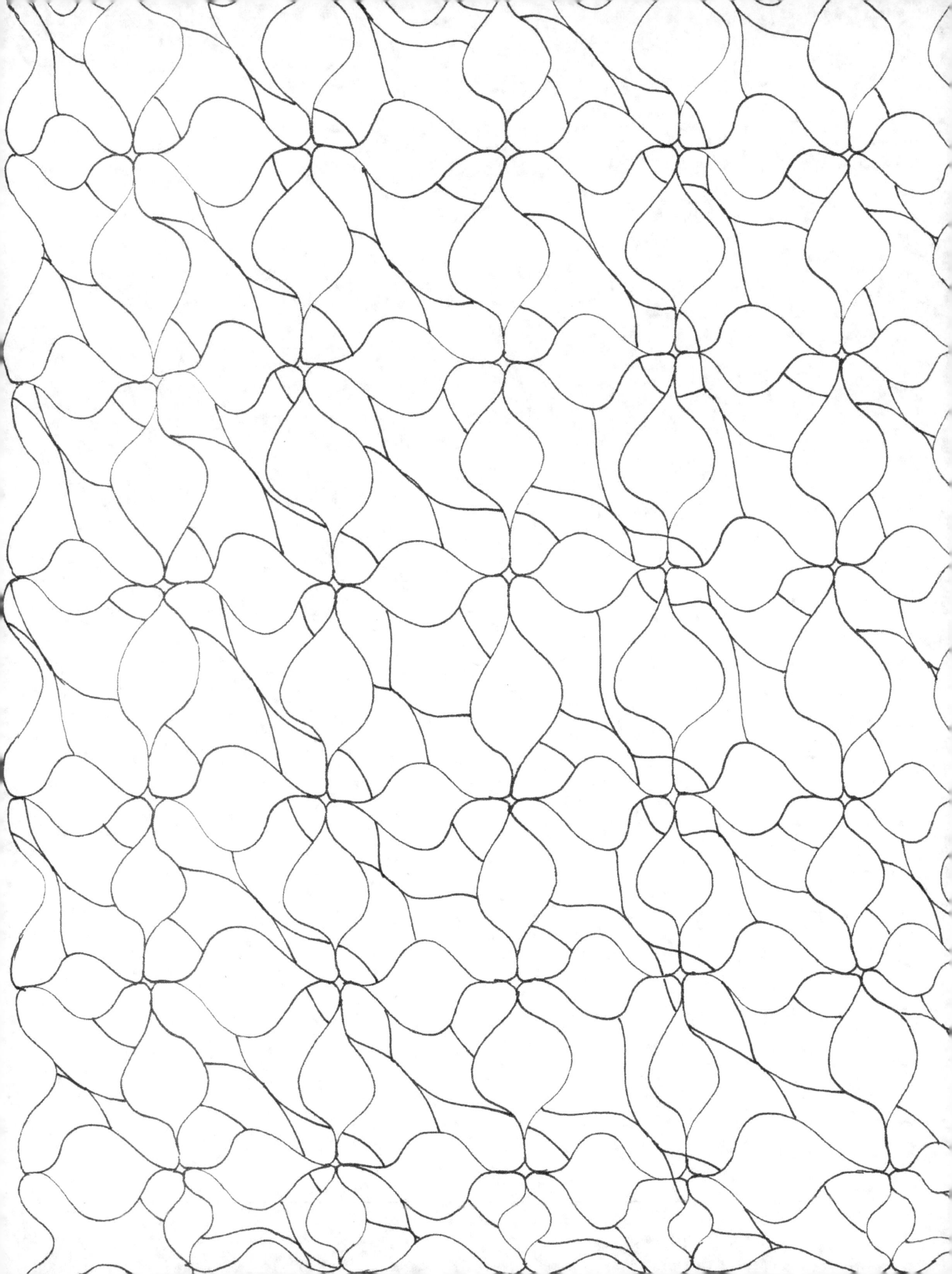

# Doodle Space

# Bicycle Headbadges and the Art of Doodling

I met Jeff Connor, author of *A Cycling Lexicon: Bicycle Headbadges from a Bygone Era* published by Gingko Press, at Kzoo Book's Author Hop & Merry Mitten 2017 event. I was there to sign copies of my first Hoodles book and meet some of the other local authors. From Jeff, I learned that bicycles used to be produced with unique badges made out of various types of metals that identified the business that produced them. As I paged through the photographs in his book, I found the artistic design of the headbadges unique and interesting. Jeff agreed to let me use some of the designs in his book as ideas for doodles in my next adult coloring book. We thought it would be a great idea to cross-promote each other's work.

When I sat down to try and convert one of the headbadges into a doodle, I realized this was going to be harder than it looked. While intriguing, the photos proved challenging to convert to two-dimensional colorable designs. I was not happy with my first attempt at a hand-drawn version, but was also not willing to give up the project. I ended up tearing my photo of choice out of the book (sorry, Jeff!) and purchasing a light box from a local hobby store, figuring it might come in handy for other projects as well.

My light box is a square metal box topped with an opaque plastic cover. Inside is a very bright light. Once plugged in, you can turn the light on and use it for tracing images that are otherwise hard to see. Because the image I selected had a very dark background, I could not photocopy it and would not have been able to trace it without the help of a light box.

I traced the headbadge I selected (Mela Royal, page 211) onto a piece of plain white paper, and embellished the result into something colorable. The process was so time-consuming that I used only one design from Jeff's book, although that is not to say I won't try again with another in the future.

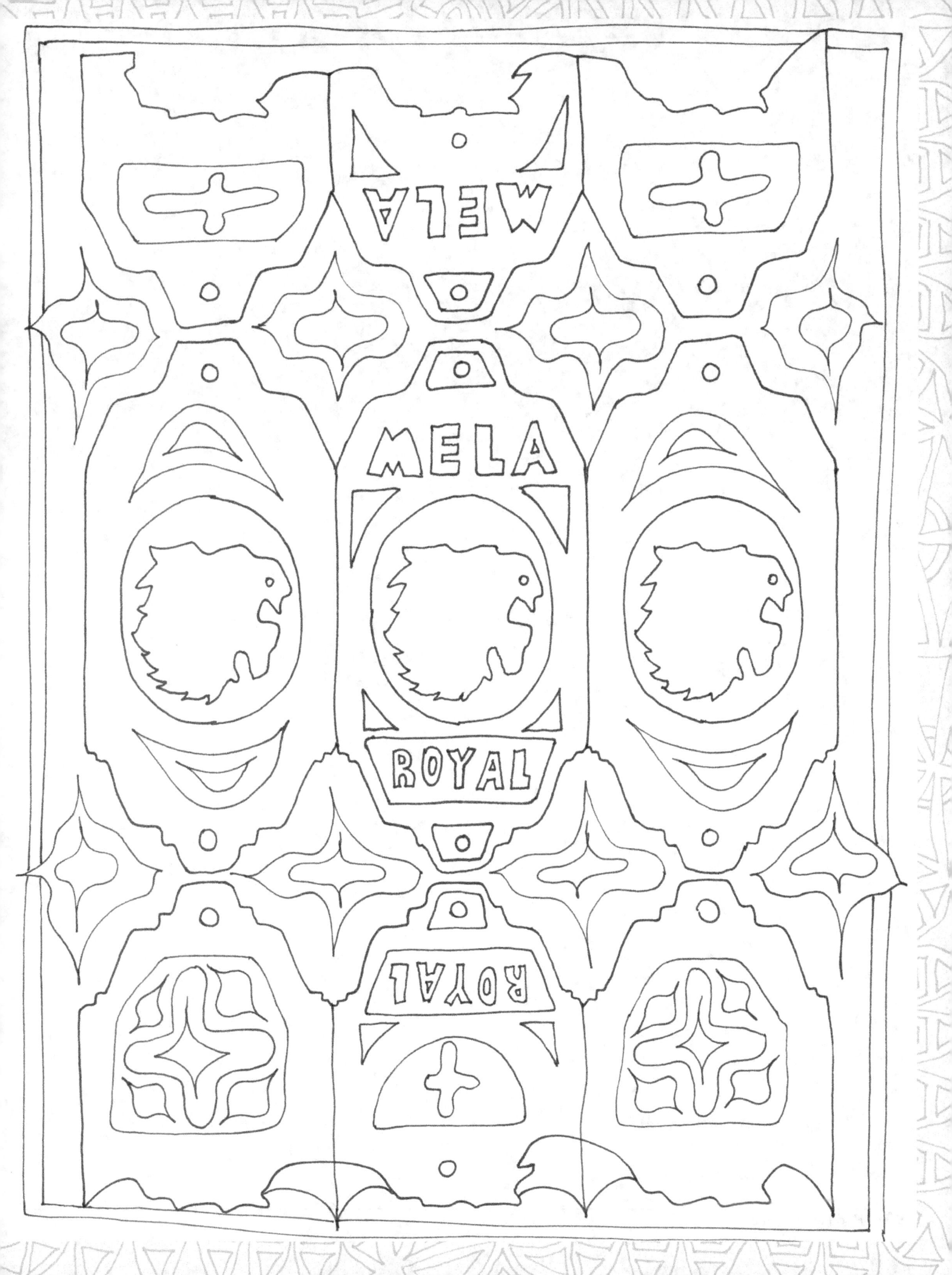

## Doodle Space

# Acknowledgments

I would like to thank my family and friends whose support and encouragement made this book possible. Special thanks to my my sister, Peggy (Margaret) Hoopingarner, my aunt, Rebecca Craft, and my friend, Debbie Eisenbise, who previewed the written parts of my book; and to those who colored doodles for my Hoodles Facebook page and the book's back cover, including Peggy, Debbie, my mother, Paula Limburg, and my daughter. Thanks to my nephew, Max Hoopingarner, for making a promotional video for my first coloring book (and promising to make one for the second!). Thanks to Michelle Bouma, Debbie Eisenbise, and Pimam Manzi for attending my ABC (Adult Bible study Coloring) group, and to my church friends, Andrea Wetzel and Karen Betten, for their enthusiasm and encouragement. Thanks to my neighbor, Norma Futrell, who colored my all my pictures and asked when the next book was coming out. Thanks to my Brondsema and Limburg relatives who purchased copies of my first coloring book. Thanks to the local Kalamazoo book stores who agreed to carry my book, including Kazoo Books, Michigan News Stand, Book Bug, and the Kalamazoo Institute of Arts gift shop. I'm looking forward to when you are able to open up again so I can come over and show you the new version in person! And finally, thanks to you, dear reader and fellow colorist, for investing in my book and allowing yourself to experience the joy of self-expression through art.

For those who are interested, I used a free app I found on the internet to convert photos to pencil sketches for parts of this book. That app can be found on https://www3.lunapic.com/editor.

Happy Hoodling!

## Doodle Space

# About The Author

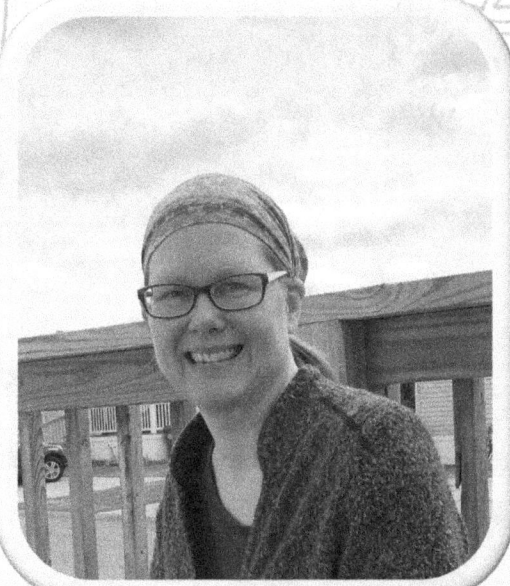

Heidi is a social worker by day and a doodler by night. Her main hobby is raising her daughter with Love and Logic principles. She also enjoys playing with Oliver (her cat), reading books (mostly digital) obtained from her local public library, planning her spring garden, and dreaming up new improvements for her home.

If you are so inclined, she would appreciate any honest feedback that will help her do an even more spectacular job the next time around. Reviews may be left on her Amazon book page.

Follow the author on Amazon to keep informed when new books come out: amazon.com/author/heidilimburg, and join her Facebook page at facebook.com/HeidiLimburgHoodles to keep in touch with other doodlers and upload samples of your colored pages. Copies of Heidi's artwork may also be posted online as part of a book review.

This book was self-published using Kindle Direct Publishing.

www.ingramcontent.com/pod-product-compliance
Lightning Source LLC
Chambersburg PA
CBHW080513220526
45465CB00006B/2470